THE RIVER

Reflections on the Times of Our Lives

Donald X. Burt, O.S.A.

A Liturgical Press Book

THE LITURGICAL PRESS
Collegeville, Minnesota

Cover design by Greg Becker.

1   2   3   4   5   6   7   8   9

Library of Congress Cataloging-in-Publication Data

Burt, Donald X.
    The river : reflections on the times of our lives / Donald
X. Burt.
        p.   cm.
    ISBN 0-8146-2477-4
    1. Meditations.   2. Christian life—Catholic authors.   I. Title.
BX2182.2.B85   1998
248.4'82—dc21   97-24743
                                                          CIP

Contents

Introduction

> "The times are bad! The times are troublesome!" This is what
> humans say. But we *are* our times. Let us live well and our
> times will be good. Such as *we* are, such are our times.
>
> *Sermon 80*, 8

Reading these words of Augustine, one is tempted to respond "That's easy for you to say; you are a saint!" But, once
we learn something about his life, it becomes clear that though
the "saying" was easy, putting it into practice in his own life
was just as hard as it is for most of us. Augustine did not have
a particularly easy life, one free of the tensions and temptations
of the ordinary person facing the world, and this perhaps explains why he has remained interesting through the ages.
Though I have great respect for those saints who seem to have
lived innocent otherworldly lives from infancy, I have never
had the gall to make them my "role-models." Too much tarnish
has gathered on my "earthen vessel" to claim such purity. Too
much "fetid water has gone under my bridge" to pretend to
their otherworldliness.

Augustine's life, on the other hand, holds out greater hope
for those of us who (as he says) have been through the furnace
and have come out half-cracked. His life experiences are simi-
lar to at least some of ours. He was not born virtuous; he had
virtue thrust upon him by the grace of God. He had to be
saved by a radical conversion and preserved by grace-instilled
perseverance. His life was far from being an arrow-straight line

to heaven. He lost the way through much of his early life, and when, finally, he discovered the right path he was never free from the temptation to jump off again or, at least, to sit down and stop making progress.

There is a good chance that when a man like that says something about life, he knows what he is talking about. Certainly Augustine knew the good and bad in human existence. Augustine knew what it was like to be driven by ambition, to be overcome by passion, to experience depression. He knew how it felt to win at games, to have lots of friends, to be deeply in love with another human being, to succeed at work, to have a son. He knew what it was like to have a mother die before she could enjoy many years of his "straightening out his life." He knew what it was like to have a dearly loved son die while still young. And finally, in his later years he knew how it felt to be so consumed by daily work that there was little quiet time for contemplation or resting.

When Augustine proclaimed "We make our times!" he was not acting as a Pollyanna. He was not telling his friends that they could make their lives better by simply thinking that they were better. His ailing body proved that mind could not control the dissolution of matter; his memory of personal tragedy would not allow him to believe that tragedy can be avoided by good thinking. He would agree with the simple sad fact that we cannot do away with death or destruction or failure or the loss of a love by thinking. All we *can* do is deal with it.

The only truth about this life that he was trying to convey was that if we are good people, nothing else will matter in the long run. Being good now means that we will have a good eternity. Whether we have good times just now is partially the "luck of the draw." "Will I be sick? Will I be rich? Will I be loved?" The answer to such questions depends on factors beyond our control. But having said that, it remains true that, though we cannot control all of the times of our lives, we can develop healthy attitudes towards them. We can make our times a bit more bearable by understanding how this moment of our lives, indeed, how *all* the moments of our lives fit into the scheme of things.

Augustine uses many analogies to present this broad picture of every human's life, but perhaps the most instructive is the image of human life as a river. It starts with the fact that our life is surrounded by eternity. The time through which we live out our mature lives is like a high plateau that drops off on all sides into an infinite space below. We begin our lives on the mountains at the very center of this plateau. Touched by the heavens, a tiny stream of life is formed and courses downward growing in strength and size until it splashes out as a mature river on the plain below. This river is our mature life, and it makes its way with many twists and turns across the broad expanse until finally it plummets like a Great Waterfall into the eternity beyond.

At each stage of our history here on earth, it is important for us to understand our times, to face up to them, to enjoy or cope with them as the situation allows. The pages that follow are an attempt to achieve some understanding of some of the moments of human life. The reflections are sometimes personal, sometimes suggested by words of Augustine.

Hopefully some of them will strike a resonant chord in the heart of the reader. After all, though we may take very different paths down the mountain and across the plain, there is not that much difference between our rivers, the lives we live on our way to eternity. We all are fluid beings of infinite possibility, and we are all going to the same place: the edge of the plateau where time and eternity meet.

The River

1

> As a torrent is formed from the rains and eventually breaks through its narrow banks and runs roaring down the slopes until it finally finishes its course, so it is with each of our lives. This passing state that we call our lives roars and rushes away.
>
> *Commentary on Psalm 109, 20*

Now that I am in my seventh decade, I have come to appreciate Augustine's river-image for human life. In a very real sense a "lot of water has passed under my bridge" and it does seem on some bad days that my life was "all downhill" after birth. Luckily, my Christian faith puts a happier meaning on this last somber saying. It tells me that, in truth, I began in the heavens rather than from earth, that I was loved into life by a God who wanted me and parents who cherished me.

Developing Augustine's theme, there is some truth in saying that our lives began in the clouds like tiny raindrops falling on a high mountain, at first forming a trickle of no moment, eventually becoming a young torrent, gathering life and force as it rushed madly down the slope towards an unforeseen future, twisted this way and that by a seemingly uncontrollable force, the force of a new life suddenly unchained. We were FREE (or so we thought) as we plunged exuberantly out of childhood onto the broad plateau at the mountain's foot, that flat plain that was to be the place where we would live out our mature years. We were FREE to go wheresoever we wished, unfettered by a long history or any established channel.

For most of us that freedom was quickly lost. As our lives entered their middle years the gushing undirected flood became diminished by dams and subsidiary streams. New responsibilities channeled our strength; new loves arose to claim our attention and focus our affection. As we grew older, the excitement of being wanted and being needed died down. A tiredness grew along with accomplishment. We sought quiet pools on which to restfully float, but we found that we were still threatened by crashing currents and hidden rocks, anxieties and fears that could not be easily escaped because we were confined now by the steep canyon walls of our now developed history, our established responsibilities, our weakness hardened by habit, by the limits of our proven strengths. We suddenly came to the realization that what we "would be" was no different than what we "were" and that there was little anyone could do about it. The track that we would follow through time was figuratively "set in stone" and all we could do was deal with it, put up with it, and (hopefully) sometimes even enjoy it.

When finally we come to our later years, we find a certain freedom. Like a great river coming to its end, we can move slowly and spread out as far as we wish. There is no one who can, or is even interested, in saying "nay" to us. We are no longer contained by the expectations of others. We broaden our lessening flood into shallows, thin experiences of simple things that will easily evaporate as we plunge over the Great Falls ahead. Our lives now have great length and great breadth but less earthy substance. We have become ephemeral to the world around us. Though others are too kind to say it, they consider us to be "history." But we know better. We can feel power deep inside ourselves, the hidden gravity that has pulled us towards the brink of the plateau that has supported the course of our flow for so many years. Now it carries us towards eternity no longer encumbered by the detritus of time.

Now I can see that my life is indeed like a flowing river of moments coursing from an ever decreasing future, through the "eye-blink" that is the present, to an ever increasing past. It is like an hour glass wide at the top and bottom where the tiny shards of sand that are the moments of my life flow faster and faster through the narrow stem of my present.

Only as you get older can you get a sense of the whole stream. Looking back you can see the reality experienced, the twists and turns, the flood and famine, the rushing rapids and the quiet pools that a long river passes through. Looking ahead you can see nothing but possibility. Perhaps that explains why the attention span of the young is so short. They have little to remember and thus nothing to give context to the present, nothing to serve as a basis for hopeful anticipation of the future.

Perhaps too that is why the maladies that destroy memory are so frightening. Looking at the vacant eyes of poor souls whose memory has departed, one sadly realizes that the stream of life has rushed through their consciousness, leaving nothing behind but a certain clinging dampness on the walls. Like babies they have lost a sense of self. They cannot see who they are because they have forgotten when they have been.

Considering the alternatives (being young or being dead), being old is not too bad if your body is not too troublesome and if you have a good memory. Once I was told that you need to be sixty to master the wisdom of metaphysics, that science that takes the widest view of reality. Now I can see the truth in that assertion. It does indeed take a length of years of living and remembering and hoping before you can discover how things really are, how things fit together, what is truly important and not important.

As we humans float quietly into the shortening future, we have a chance to see the present in a clearer light and to better understand the past. We are coming closer to that moment when all that is past and future dissolves into that eternal present which awaits us at just the other side of the Falls. Anticipating that eternity, our time suddenly becomes clearer.

Infancy: The Beginning 2

> A sign of divine love is that even after Adam's sin God allowed humans the happiness of creating children, making something exist that would be a thing of beauty and an adornment of earth.
>
> *On Free Will,* 3.20.55

We existed through eternity in the mind of God. We come into time like tiny tears of divine love falling upon the heights, eventually coalescing into streams trickling down the mountain towards the plain below. In the womb we are only minute droplets at first, wee small bits of mostly liquid life absolutely dependent on the kindness of strangers, those strange creatures that we will later call "Mama" and "Dada." We exit the womb with a cry, perhaps (as Augustine suggests) because we already see the frightening swirls and eddies and hidden rocks of our future river-life.

Of course Augustine expressed his somber view as a forty year old bruised human being, and it probably reflects more middle-age feelings looking back rather than infant worries looking forward. Like most of us he could not remember much further back than his early school days (where apparently he was beaten rather frequently). Possibly his feelings about his infancy would have been more sunny had he been able to remember how he truly felt as a baby.

Experience with babies of my acquaintance leads me to believe that my own first years were fairly pleasant. Of course I was one of the lucky ones, born healthy in a family that seemed to want me. Like most other babies, I probably exited the womb with a slap, but this was for medical rather than symbolic reasons. Forcing a healthy cry is the most direct way to get babies to start breathing. Once we master that trick, we infant humans quickly doze off in peace, resting for the life-journey that lies ahead. Our first waking experience is of hunger and we find immediate satisfaction at the soft breast of one who loves us. We sleep, we eat, and we wake and soon begin to smile. And why not? Never again will peace be so easily attained.

As infants we are already on the road to a sometimes difficult life but right now we have found rest, nourishment, and love. We are still but tiny streams, pure, innocent, with no mistakes made, no guilt, no remorse. The world seems just fine and we laugh frequently. Of course we do cry sometimes too, but usually for pragmatic reasons. We have yet to master fax or e-mail or even language, and yelling is about the only alternative we have for attracting attention. It will get little respect later on, but right now it seems accepted and it certainly does work. Only later, when we have developed powers of language, will communication be a problem. Only then will we complain "No one understands me!" A crying baby's wants are simple and are understood very quickly by those who love them.

All things considered, it is my opinion that for most of us, being a baby was just fine. It was only when we became kids that our troubles began. Then we began to have a remembered past and a recognizable future. Perhaps that is the secret of the joy of the infant. It has only a present. It does not have a past to regret nor a future to worry about. At breakfast it does not remember the argument at last night's dinner nor does it worry whether it will get any lunch. Its world is the world of the present. Every moment is new and each one is relished, enjoyed, and embraced. Only later will this trickle of humanity be afraid to plunge into its present lest it become too "involved." Only later will it begin to worry about its future and be sorry for its past. Just now it is able to be thoroughly an infant, rejoicing in what is happening *now*.

What a shame that we humans can't seem to make such innocent joy last! What a shame that we are not able to repeat the sentiments of our unremembered infant days on every day of our lives, crying out in glee: "Just now I feel GOOD! Just now I am with my love. Just now I have accomplished something I am proud of. Just now the day is fine and life is interesting and I am not afraid."

When the old look at the very young, they do it perhaps with some envy. Infants seem to come from heaven like a spring shower, and they romp through the sparkling waters of their infancy with no thought of trouble or sorrow or pain. Their world is a world of brightness and joy. Faith tells us that this is the sort of world that awaits all of us beyond the Great Falls that mark our death. When we look at an infant's present, we are looking at our future. Perhaps that is why, when we see a happy baby, most of us smile.

Adolescence   3

> I was in love with love. The desires of my flesh were like the
> mists rising from a swamp, clouding my heart's vision so that I
> could not distinguish between true love and lust. I was 16 and
> driven almost crazy by all my desires.
>
> *Confessions,* 1.1-2

Growing up is not an easy thing to do. Especially when you are on the verge of being classed as an "adult." When we were little, no one expected much of us and everyone seemed to like us. No one depended on us for a living; no one called for our single-minded love. We had many friends; but they were just for play. We did not need to be serious; and no one took us seriously. We had not yet moved from being "cute" to being "silly." We had not yet heard those ominous words: "Why don't you grow up!"

When we were babies we were like little streams, and we gave pleasure to others with our pleasing gurgles. We were allowed to play among the trees and flowers, free of all responsibility. We did not have to worry about where we were going. As we meandered down the mountain towards maturity, our course was fixed by the stable channel that contained us, the experience and decisions of our elders. The force that moved us was the gravity of our growing. We had little to say about whether or not we would grow bigger and become more conscious, and thereby be held responsible for what we were.

All this changed when we reached the bottom of the mountain of our youth and faced the broad plateau on which we would live out our maturity. The flat plain before us seemed a land of infinite opportunity. There was no great force driving us, nor were there any fixed paths to follow. We had to decide to take that first tentative step towards being an adult. We had to decide the direction that the rest of our life would take. We were adolescents and people had come to expect us to move ahead on our own.

There was some protection in our need to "go to school." Like infancy, this too was something like a safe haven, where few decisions were required and where the measure for success or failure was laid out for us. The only threat was the possibility of finally "failing" something (we had never failed at being at least a "passable" baby), but even this could be avoided by selective course selection and tears at the appropriate time. Unfortunately for most of us, the extension of childhood through "studenthood" cannot last forever, despite the availability of graduate courses, post-graduate grants, and (when all else is exhausted) self-improvement programs. Eventually most of us are forced to move out on the terrifying plain of personal responsibility. Finally we must be a "grown-up" and take charge of our lives.

When, as adolescents, we first tried to take charge, we sometimes found that our lives were out of control. There was a power inside us that we could not seem to manage. We grew in body and spirit in a somewhat disorderly fashion, quite different (we thought) from the way our friends grew. They seemed to "have it all together," to be smart, to be beautiful.

We, on the other hand, were disorganized, dumb, and infected with terminal ugliness. It seemed that we were condemned to be either a small creek or a raging torrent in a land where everyone else flowed through life in a normal way. Everyone else seemed to be "size medium" while we tried to cope with a body and spirit that seemed either extra-small or extra-large.

We were conscious of powerful tides within us that rose and fell without permission, and sometimes in the most embarrassing ways. We tried to be cool, but a new flame burned within. The heat and fire that later would drive the course of our mature flow, the majestic broad current of the prime of our lives, was beginning to rise in us, and we were not sure how to direct it. Indeed, like Augustine at sixteen, we were not even sure that we wanted to control it. By our lives we proved his view that, as humans grow, they move from ignorance to wisdom through an intermediate stage of foolishness (*Against Julian*, 5.4.18).

Still, the adolescent years can be a good and exciting time. It is a time when we approach the high tide of our river's flow, when both our body and our spirit are bursting with unexpended energy. For the first time we are called upon to go out on our own, and there are no rules forbidding us to strike out in directions quite different from the channels that define the lives of others. There are no responsibilities that stand in the way of our seeing new sights, hearing new sounds, exploring the unexplored. Under the providence of God there are unlimited paths to the edge of the plateau where this life ends, and one path is as good as another as long as it follows the laws of loving God and neighbor, which are the keys to eternal success.

In many ways human life resembles the broad deltas that mark the end of the great rivers of this world. Their many streams wander off from the main channel just before they disappear into the great sea beyond. So too for each of us, though we may for a time twist and turn apparently far from the normal course that humans have defined as a "sensible" life, we all end in the same way, tumbling into eternity. Still, it is hard to see this when we stand at the beginning of our journey across the broad plateau. To be able to go "anywhere" carries with it the fear of ending up nowhere. At such a time we can understand the feelings behind Augustine's prayer:

> How mixed up I get, Jesus! And how sad my poor spirit becomes when it tries to find rest without you. It feels all alone in its little place on earth. It turns this way and that in its tiny life only to find itself more uncomfortable. Only you, Lord, can bring it peace.
>
> *Confessions,* 6.16

Finding Self   **4**

> If by the word "abyss" we mean something that has great depth, is it not proper to describe the human heart as an abyss? Can you not see that this inner "self" is hidden even from the one whose "self" it is?
>
> *Commentary on Psalm 41,* 13

At the beginning of Augustine's life as a baptized Christian he wrote these words: "O God, you who are always the same, let me know myself, let me know you" (*Soliloquies,* 2.1.1). The order of his prayer is significant. It shows that he believed that he could not stand face to face with his God without first standing face to face with himself.

However, the proposed order of investigation does not imply that he thought it any easier to discover "self" than to discover God. In many ways it is more difficult. When a person comes to know God, the work is done mostly by God. To know "self" is mostly the work of the human, supported (but not forced), by the grace of God. Moreover when one comes to "see" God, there is no problem in accepting what one sees. God is all-good. There is nothing despicable or frightening in his nature. We may have trouble accepting what we must do with our lives after seeing God, but the "seeing" itself is a pleasant experience. This is not always the case when we honestly look at ourselves and see ourselves for what we are. It may be difficult to accept that (using Augustine's descriptive analogies) we are as "fragile as glass" and as "flimsy as spider webs." It may be difficult for our pride to realize that we would not make very good gods, that indeed we are not even very reputable human beings.

Faced with the challenges of our imperfections, we may be tempted to go back over our résumé and fictionalize the facts a bit, changing our birthday, adding to our intelligence, explaining away our failed loves and failed projects as being someone else's fault, rejecting the truth that we do not have an inferiority complex, that we truly *are* inferior.

Even apart from the uncomfortable things we may find there, the self remains a difficult mystery to unravel and understand. Augustine remarked once that it was easier to count the hairs on his head than the feelings in his heart (*Confessions*, 4.14). The danger of unpleasant discoveries leads to procrastination. To use another Augustinian analogy, people with dirty houses are likely to spend most of their time outside wandering through the noise and bustle of the city square, rather than coping with the filth inside the door of their own home (*Commentary on Psalm 33*, 2.8).

It is easy to put off self-analysis because it does not force itself upon us. We are not born with a passion for such awareness and I am not sure that we have much of it through the first years of life. I for one do not remember much of anything of my infancy, indeed little beyond 6 A.D. (6 Anno Donaldo). My knowledge of the infancy of others leads me to believe that they too begin life mostly confused about their identity, apparently thinking that their thumb is a tasty morsel for eating rather than a personal appendage for grabbing. I am told that in my early years I did respond to the name "Donald" but, like the old dog "Buck," I had little awareness of the "me" that the name represented.

As we move through the later years of childhood we do finally come to some perception of who we are, and mostly we do not try to hide the fact. We are "little people" and it is somewhat enjoyable. At the same time, it can be frightening. Everything seems so much bigger and higher, and we are anxious to grow up and move beyond "being cute" to "being taken seriously." Only later do we glamorize our childhood and develop a nostalgia for being a kid again, a nostalgia not shared by the old Augustine who remarked that, given the choice, he truly would much rather die than go back and start life over again (*City of God,* 21.14).

The difficulties in looking at ourselves and accepting ourselves continue throughout all of our ages. As adolescents we sometimes fear looking at ourselves lest we find something that is unlovable. We look to others and try to make ourselves what they want us to be. As young adults we sometimes will not face up to the fact that the one we love does not love us, that the career we truly desire is far beyond our abilities. In our middle years we must deal with unrealized dreams, the awareness that, despite all our efforts, we have not made the progress in love and life that we promised ourselves, and that we are quickly getting beyond the point where we can start over with new adventures. Finally, when we are old it is sometimes difficult to look at our wizened self and accept the fact that our past is longer than our future, that others are now responsible for the world and are likely to get along very well, "Thank you very much," without our advice. Looking at our diminished life, we may be forced to cope with the fact that, though we may still be loved, as far as our earthly career is concerned we are definitely "on the shelf," and no one is reaching to take us down. We have become a pleasing heirloom, safely tucked away in the china closet with all the other curios of times past.

When we finally discover our true self, we may be unpleasantly shocked, but also we may be pleasantly surprised. Whatever the result, it is a task that must be undertaken for ourselves, our neighbor, and our God. We must do it for ourselves because our only chance at happiness is through being what we are, not what we pretend to be. If we are made to be happy as a human being, we can never be happy as a god or as a brute animal. We must do it for our neighbor because we can only go out to them with love if we have a place to go out from. We cannot love others if we do not love ourselves as we are, with all our beauty marks and blemishes. Finally, we must do it to discover God because our "self" is the primary place where God reveals himself to us this side of death.

In truth, seeing the good and bad in ourselves is a daunting experience and creates a new challenge. Our sadness at the bad and our joy at the good cannot be allowed to get out of hand. Our deficiencies must not lead to depression and despair; our virtues must not lead to pride. In the midst of our sadness about our defects, we must remember that, as Augustine wrote long ago, "God does not make useless human beings" (*On Freedom of the Will*, 3.23.66), and therefore even our decrepit "self" has a part to play in God's scheme of things. In the midst of our joy over our gifts, we must remember that we are still "cracked," and not even God expects us to be perfect in this present world. Once we see ourselves and accept ourselves as we are, we then become a special place of God in the world, a place where he can reveal himself to us even now.

But first we must withdraw from the noisy turmoil outside and settle down quietly in the silence of our newly discovered self.

The Babble Outside: The Quiet Within   **5**

> Speak here inside me Lord, because only you always tell me the truth. I shall leave all the noisy world outside and retire to my own little room deep inside my heart and there I will sing my love song to you.
>
> *Confessions*, 12.16

On this river that is our life there is so much NOISE, shouting conflicting voices screaming constantly about what God is like, what God hates, who is evil and who is good, who is damned and who is saved, quoting scripture passages to prove a point, ignoring the context, emphasizing *this* word or *that* word, ignoring the fact that the WHOLE scripture taken together is *THE WORD* and that shouting this phrase or that phrase to suit their present purposes makes it impossible for anyone to hear the simple message of the Lord, never shutting up, running on forever and ever . . . like this sentence.

Deafened by the babble outside, we would truly like to turn inside ourselves, to withdraw into solitude of "self" where we have at least a chance to hear God telling us how to lead the blessed life here and hereafter, telling us: "Don't hate anyone. Don't waste yourself on trivialities. Never despair of reaching heaven. Never be afraid to say 'I'm sorry.'"

On most days it is hard to hear such divine whispers because we are deafened by the rushing waters of our lives, the passing events and the shouting people that surround us. We have the "Pilate" problem. When Jesus stood in the public square face to face with Pilate, Pilate could not hear him because of the shouting crowd. It was only when Pilate took Jesus inside, into his own private house, that the Roman was able to truly hear Jesus telling him, "Indeed, I *am* a king!" Who knows? Perhaps Jesus never would have been crucified if Pilate had kept talking to him in the quiet of his own private quarters. It is hard to kill a God when you are looking into his eyes in a quiet room. But outside the voice of God was drowned out by the frenzy of the crowd. Pilate was overcome with the noise and the needs of his external world. He was swept along by the screams of the crowds, shouting fallacies often repeated in human history: *This* prophet is always right but *that* prophet is always wrong! If you join *our* group, you are certainly saved! If you do not join *our* group, you are certainly lost!

When we search for salvation in the midst of the babble surrounding us, we sometimes will join any new group that promises security. Sometimes we simply give up trying to find answers and give in to what Augustine called the "concupiscence of the eyes," a vain curiosity about inconsequential things. We spend all our time peering into the boats of everyone else (especially those odd enough to be "talk-show" celebrities) and are left with no time at all to concentrate on our own destiny, our own weakness and strength.

It is truly a shame when this happens. Perhaps television lives are more interesting than ours, but they are not *ours*. Our little boat may be more humble and more boring than the vessels of others, but at least it is *our* boat. It is *this* life that we must deal with because it the only vessel that will carry us over the Great Falls at the end of our time. It is the *only* place where Jesus can find us and be with us as we whirl through the rest of our days.

Living a life constantly outside of ourselves may be more interesting, but it also can be a burden. Augustine once told a friend that he thought it easier to bear the difficult life and storms of the wilderness than the things humans must suffer or fear in the "busyness" of the world (*Letter 95*, 4). To another he wrote:

> I simply cannot taste and enjoy the truly good things of eternity as long as I have no relief from the care and work of today. Believe me, one must have many withdrawals of oneself from the turmoil of passing events before it can be said: "I fear nothing!"

Letter 10, 2

What Augustine is telling us is that each must find her/his own hermitage and the only place where this exists in this noisy world is within one's own consciousness. Only in this inner self can I find a personal solitude hidden from everyone else. Outside, the world is driven hither and yon by storms and troubles. It is only inside that I can reflect on my convictions about life and death, God and myself, my loves and my hates. It is only there that I can find peaceful rest in hope. It is a secret place where only I and God dwell, a place where God will reveal to me what I have kept hidden, a place where I can experience the only valuable praise, the praise that I and every human being has from God (*Sermon 47*, 14.23).

It is hard for any human being to achieve this quiet. The uproar of the world keeps calling us from our inner sanctuary, demanding that we look back to this world rather than look forward to the world to come (*Sermon 105*, 5.7). Withdrawal from the noisy crowd is especially difficult for one who is concerned (as we all must be) about helping others to come to God. Unless we join them in their lives, we cannot reach them. But by involving ourselves in the passing good things of such lives we come to enjoy them, and this creates a new bond restraining us from returning into the quiet within (*Letter 95*, 2). Indeed, the more we become attached to the noisy world outside, the more we may come to fear withdrawing to the silence within, frightened that it will become a prison from which we cannot escape. Only through a habit of quiet solitude can we come to see it for what it is: an Eden with no walls, a world of reverie where anything is possible, a safe place where for a while one can sit and watch the noisy world outside.

What Augustine said of his own life is true for every human being:

> We truly are thirsting for a taste of everlasting peace but our thoughts are still twisted and turned in all directions by the ebb and flow of time. If only we could seize our spirits and make

them stay still for a moment! Then perhaps we could glimpse for an instant the splendor of an eternity that is forever still.

Confessions, 11.11

God in Us 6

If only the uproar in our flesh could be silenced, if the sounds of the land and air and sea and the very heavens could be silenced too, if the human spirit itself could come to a quiet place beyond its thoughts, dreams, and imaginations . . . perhaps then God would speak face to face with us.

Confessions, 9.10.25

The words above are from a conversation Augustine had with his mother, Monica, immediately after they had enjoyed an intense experience of God. Neither of them enjoyed such ecstasy again. Monica died soon after and Augustine went on to live forty more years deeply involved in the affairs of this world. Like most of the rest of us, the presence of God experienced by Monica and Augustine through the rest of their lives was much quieter, perhaps manifested only through an inner peace in the midst of external turmoil, a quiet hope in depressing times, a conviction that the past was forgiven and that the future would be guided by God's providential care.

To have even such a modest awareness of God would satisfy most of us. In our journey down the river that is our life we think anxiously about what is before us, about what we are facing now, about the sometimes terribly stupid events of our past, and we look to the heavens and cry "Where are you God?" We may not even be too sure whom we are addressing; all we know is that we want to get in contact with *something,* or better *someone,* who can make sense of our situation and be with us as we make our way towards the Great Falls.

At such times of searching for God it is good for us to remember the advice often repeated by Augustine: "If you are
seeking a place where holiness dwells, seek it within yourself"
(*Commentary on the Gospel of John,* 15.25). Standing on the
deck of our little boat, frantically searching the heavens for a
divine presence, we need to go into the little cabin that houses
our inner "self." There, if we are patient, we shall discover the
God who waits for us.

One thing is certain, we will never find him by rushing
around outside looking for some foreign place where he dwells
or searching for some book (even this one) or some guru who
will bring him to us. To use an Augustinian analogy, our "self"
is like the center of a circle, and it is the only point from which
we can see, in some unified way, the universe that surrounds us.
To the extent that we rush away from that center to the mul-
tiple places and events on the edges of the circumference, we
lose the ability to find that unity that is God. God is not at the
fringes of our life. He is at the very center and only by returning to that center that is our "self" can we see ourselves and the
universe through the eyes of God. Only by returning to our
"self" can we find the God who will help us "put it all together"
(*On Order,* 1.2.3).

Augustine believed that this experience of God "in us" is
possible for every human being precisely because it is in the
human "self" that one finds the most perfect image of God in
creation. It is because God lives within us that our fragile existence is supported, that we have the great power to love, that we
can discover the secrets of the universe. Jesus-God within us is
our teacher, a private tutor who reveals the truths that each one
needs to successfully manage life and death. Christ speaks inside the cabin of our boat but we cannot hear him if we stay
outside amidst the roar of the passing crowd. Augustine learned
from his own experience that: . . . "It is hard to find Christ in
a crowd. God is discovered only in solitude. A crowd is consumed with noisy talking; the vision of God requires a quiet
seclusion" (*Commentary on the Gospel of John,* 17.11.2).

To find God "in us" we must not only go inside ourselves, we must also not expect too much in the way of dramatic effects from the meeting. Sometimes we act like those characters in the play *Waiting for Godot*. We sit on our haunches waiting for some miraculous, dramatic "coming of the Lord." We sit on the deck of our little boat (never thinking of going inside the cabin) reading the Scripture story of the transfiguration and we say to ourselves:

> Oh, if only I could have been there! If only God would come in all his glory as I flow through the course of my life! If only I could see him *now* as I will see him in eternity! If only, I could see him as Peter, and James, and John saw him on that mountain, *then* my life would be different, *then* the waters of my river life would be smooth and pleasant!

It is admittedly a nice dream, but it is far from the reality of life, and indeed far from the reality of the scripture story. We know, for example, that seeing Jesus on the mountain did not stop Peter from running away on Holy Thursday, and it did not stop him from running away some years later when he was threatened with martyrdom in Rome. Having seen Jesus in his youth did not make the old man John's pain any less as he was carried about on a stretcher mumbling the same words over and over, as old men sometimes do. And, finally, I suspect that having seen Jesus on the hill of transfiguration did not make James feel any better when sometime later, as the soon-to-be first apostolic martyr, he was thrown from the parapet of the Temple in Jerusalem.

Once they left the mountain of transfiguration, the most important thing for the three apostles was not that they had seen Jesus in his glory, but that he had walked back down that mountain with them to be *with* them through the rest of the days of their ordinary life. If they had spent the rest of their days on this river of life waiting for another dramatic revelation of God, they would indeed have missed the boat. They would have missed knowing that Jesus was indeed in the *same* boat with them as they floated through the ordinary days of their sometimes uneventful lives.

And so too with us, if we spend all of our time scanning the heavens "waiting for God" to come in some dramatic way, we will never see that he is now in us and with us in our ordinary days. If in the midst of sickness we set our minds on seeing God only in a miraculous cure, we will miss seeing the God who is with us in our illness, helping us to bear up under the sometimes pain and sometimes fear and sometimes depression that darkens our days of illness. If we spend all of our time waiting for Jesus to come and embrace us on some glorious height, we may forget that sometimes he comes to us in the love of a cherished human lover, that he reaches out to embrace us through the human arms of those who, beyond all explanation, love us deeply.

Just now the plan of God is not that we should peek into his world; rather it is that he should live in us in our world, to be with us in our innermost "self" as we continue our journey through those Great Falls, when finally we shall stand before him face to face. It is true that just now we cannot see him too clearly, but that is only because he is *in* us.

I. God with Us: A Divine Parent   7

> O God, you alone are always present, even to those who separate themselves from you. If only they would be converted to you, they would discover that you are in the hearts of all who accept you and ask for your help.
>
> *Confessions*, 5.2

As we make our way down the river of life, great thinkers tell us that God exists. But we still feel alone. This intellectual revelation does no more for our loneliness than learning that billions of other humans share our life-journey. "Aloneness" is not cured by knowing that somebody else exists; it is cured only by the conviction that there is someone who cares that *we* exist.

Proving to someone that God exists does not prove that God cares about *us,* or indeed that he cares about those billion others who share our times. The classical proofs for God's existence are logical but they are cold. They have never made anyone feel better or less alone. It is fine to have a "divine watchmaker" to explain the order of the universe, and an "uncaused cause" to explain its existence; but what we really need is a *friend*.

After thirty years of searching, Augustine came to the conclusion that the only way to know God as friend was through faith. Reading the Old and New Testament stories about God, especially those about Jesus Christ, he came to realize that those pages were directed precisely at *him*, that the way God in the Old Testament dealt with the chosen people and the way that the New Testament Christ treated his friends and acquaintances was the way God was related to him right now. Through his developing faith Augustine was able to know that he had not only a friend in high places; he had a lover.

Suddenly the Scripture pages became a love letter from God, each page communicating a different truth about his divine friend. With this insight he reread the story of creation and found there the comforting message that the reason why God placed the first humans in a fruit-filled garden was that he wanted to protect and cultivate *them*. God became for Augustine something like a warm-hearted farmer who does not simply plant new crops year after year, letting them fend for themselves thereafter. God protects and cultivates whatever he brings into existence. Thus, when God creates us as human beings, he "continues to nourish and guard us so that we may be healthy and happy" (*A Literal Commentary on Genesis*, 8.10.23).

Such warm concern for each individual seems closer to the passion of a parent than the affection of a friend. God comes to us not as a stranger who meets us sometime later in life and becomes an acquaintance. God is more like a loving parent who is with us from the very first moment of our existence. Indeed, the Creator becomes both a father and mother for us. He is father because he creates us, calls us to his service, directs us, and governs us. He is mother in that he cherishes us and feeds us and nurses us. Commenting on the words of the psalmist, "Though my father and mother forsake me, yet will the Lord receive me" (Ps 27.10), Augustine compares the grief of separation that occurs in human relationships and the wonder of God's everlasting presence to every human being: "Mortals give place to mortals. Children are born to human parents but their parents must eventually leave them. But the God who created me shall never leave me nor can I ever be separated from him" (*Commentary on Psalm 26/2,* 18).

God may be closer to us than our earthly parents, but what sort of parent is he? Unfortunately not every human parent remains a lifetime friend of their child. Augustine believed that the two stories from scripture that best describe what God (our *divine* parent) is like are the stories of the prodigal son and the good Samaritan. The message of the two stories is clear. God is a parent who is always willing to open the doors of his house to any of his wandering children. God is a person who will pick up a wounded stranger left alone by the side of a road, help him heal, and finally adopt him as a beloved child (*Questions on the Gospels,* 2.33; *Sermon 131,* 6.6).

"I shall never be separated from God": this was the most important fact about life discovered by Augustine from his faith. It told him that in this beautiful world of land and sea and sky, he was the most precious creation of all. In truth it is a world made from nothing, a world in which each human being is held in existence by a tenuous thread, but it is formed by an infinite being who wants everything good for his fragile creations. It is a world in which God walks the streets as friend, doctor, and parent.

There can be no "aloneness" on the river of life for one who shares the passionate faith of Augustine because that faith shouts the message: "Wherever you go on earth, however long you remain, the Lord is close to you. So don't worry about anything. The Lord is nearby" (*Sermon 171,* 5).

II. God With Us: A Divine Brother   **8**

> Many people of advanced age, when they have no children of their own, will adopt a child. But when parents have an only child of their own, they rejoice because they know that their child will not have to share their inheritance with anyone else. This is the way humans act; but God acts differently. He sent his one and only begotten Son into this world so that he might share his heavenly home with adopted brothers and sisters.
>
> *Commentary on the Gospel of John,* 2.13.1

The world will never be so good that evil could not appear to disrupt our peace; the world will never be so evil that everything good would ever be destroyed completely. We live mostly in twilight, never knowing if the next moment will bring everlasting night or a new dawn. We dream of making our times perfect but we know that this dream can never be fulfilled. We *are* our times and deep down inside we know that we are mixed beings, beings who frequently have good intentions, but who are also sometimes terribly dumb and driven insane with perverse desire.

Augustine never believed in the inevitable progress of the human race towards some earthly Utopia. The continuing battle between good and evil in the human heart made this impossible. One cannot have peace in a totality when all of its parts are tearing themselves apart. One cannot have a perfect city when all the citizens are cracked, and this is the situation in which the human race finds itself. Because we are mixed and mixed up beings, human history can be expected to go through cycles of war and peace, enlightenment and stupidity, altruism and selfishness, till the end of time.

It is for this reason that the appearance of Jesus Christ on the river of time was so important in the history of the race. It made possible a new destiny for individual human beings. No longer did humans have a single way to go when they plunged over the Great Falls of death. The gate to heaven was opened once again to those humans who tried their best to live decent lives. Through the appearance on earth of Jesus-God as a human being, God himself intervened in human history, living with humans and then dying for the salvation of those who wanted it.

This divine intervention gave human beings someone to hang onto, one who provided some stability in an ever-changing world. The miracle of Jesus Christ was that he gave humans a person who both moved with them through time, and yet had an unmoving base in eternity. Jesus both stands in the middle of my life as I twirl downstream towards the Falls, and he also stands firmly planted on the eternal shore beyond.

Because of the radical difference between a creation that comes from nothing and a Creator who is everything, Augustine had no doubt about the absolute "otherness," the infinite transcendence of God. But through his belief in the incarnation, the appearance of this infinite God in the person of Jesus Christ, he came to see that this ineffable infinite being was close by, indeed that Jesus-God had become our neighbor and that he did this for the unfathomable reason that this "everything" who is God did not want this "nothing" who is us to worry too much (*Sermon 171,* 3.3).

And more, Jesus-God became a human being because he did not want to be an only child. To be sure, he would always be the one and only *natural* child of the Father, sharing full divinity in perfect unity with Father and Holy Spirit, but now (having joined his divine nature to human nature) he had adopted brothers and sisters. As Augustine told the people of his congregation: "His mercy would not allow him to remain alone. It was his desire that we too should be heirs of the Father, and coheirs with himself" (*Sermon 25,* 7-8).

Augustine no doubt sometimes still felt lonely as he continued his pilgrimage through this twilight world, but he never despaired. He lived out his turbulent days consoled by the truth: "It is hard to despair of life knowing how the Son of God has bent down to help us" (*The Christian Combat,* 11.12).

Changing Times   9

Without a doubt we are older now than we were this morning because nothing stands still, nothing remains fixed in time. And thus (if we seek stability in our lives) we must turn our love to the God through whom all our times are made.

Commentary on the Gospel of John, 31.5.3

Our river is ever moving. Change is a part of our lives and it can be frightening. Once we have organized and controlled a particular period in our lives, we suddenly are thrust around a bend and find ourselves facing a whole new environment. Just when we have gotten used to being a baby, we grow up. When we finish growing up and feel happy with our new state, we begin to fall apart. Once we have accommodated to our weakening powers and made a life out of our limitations, it suddenly all comes to an end and we die. We never seem to be in control. We are always facing new challenges, always tossed this way and that by new rapids.

In the beginning we were carried by others, the warm dark womb of our mother first, then in the arms of family. There was too little of us to go out on our own. We had little identity in the eyes of others. In my mother's womb I was described simply as *the baby;* "Donald" had not yet arrived. But that soon changed. Once born, I quickly began to be blamed for what I did. I was becoming a kid.

As kids we were all activity, flitting here and there, back and forth, like water-bugs on a placid pond. We were not taken too seriously because we had little weight. We found it quite easy to run across the surface of our time with no direction and little purpose, trying this and that and then running off to something (anything) new. Older people who saw us thought it grand to be so free. But deep down inside we knew it was not grand at all. We went everywhere because we had no particular place to go. But all this changed when we became adults.

As young adults life seemed promising. We had no doubt that we could find a love of our life, but felt no pressure to do so. We had no doubt that we would find a life-work that would be satisfying and richly rewarding and were not alarmed that our present job would not be forever. But as we grew older our lives seemed to become complicated. Now middle-aged, we were more involved than ever in the lives of others, worried about growing children, caring now for those who cared for us as children, looking for new ways to express affection for an accustomed love. We worried about becoming dispensable in our work, being powerless to solve the problems of those we loved, being sick when all the world seemed to depend on us. We seemed to spend more time in the boats of others than in our own.

Eventually the current moved us through such days of finding love, building career, nurturing family. We became settled, and said to ourselves "Nothing much will change now. What *is* will be." But then we woke up one day to discover that our flowing river had changed its character once again. We had become old.

If we are lucky, this is the point where the river of our life seems to broaden and become quiet. The current still has its force. Indeed, it seems more powerful than in the days of our youth, perhaps because we have stopped paddling and are now swept along by the natural force of our diminishing time. The river moves slowly now. We are placid. We have time to think. Watching the world go by, we accept that our end is closer than our beginning. We are not disturbed by this fact. We are tired and we pray only that we will live the rest of our days with grace-filled dignity. We have become old and are swept along the last miles of life by the push of the past and the pull of the Great Falls that is our future.

Our changing life has taught us that we can never give ourselves more *time*. All time is fleeting, a precious dot of "now" in an ever-moving stream. We can relish it or endure it but never preserve it. The irresistible tides of life propel us forward. We cannot stand still. We cannot reach down and grasp a handful of glistening moments to give to a friend. In the very action of treasuring the present it becomes past, a past beyond recapturing, no matter how hard we try. In the midst of our changing times our only option is to look to the future. There is nothing else that is still to come. The future is the only gift that we can give to our loves, the promise that we shall *together* share whatever future awaits us in God's heaven.

Remembering our somewhat muddled past, looking forward to our unknown future, still torn by our changing present, we can understand the middle-aged Augustine's feelings when he said to God:

> Just now my years pass as so many sighs; only you, God, are my comfort. You are eternal; I am divided between time past and time to come. My thoughts are torn this way and that by the havoc of my changing times. And so it shall be until I am purified and melted by the fire of your love, melded forever into oneness with you.
>
> *Confessions,* 11.29

Grasping at Straws   **10**

> All beauty on this earth is created by the passing away and suc-
> cession of things. In the flow of human life every age from in-
> fancy to death has its own special glory. How absurd it would
> be for someone to wish that they could always remain a child!
> To do so would be to deny themselves the beauty that comes
> only with the other ages of human life.
>
> *83 diverse questions,* 44

If our journey down the river of this life is relatively comfortable, there is the temptation to become attached to it, to
trade in our travelboat for a houseboat so that we might settle
permanently in this pleasant present moment. It is a silly
dream because its realization is simply impossible. Like it or
not we can't stay young forever, nor can we avoid old age. Like
it or not we are rushing into our future towards the Great Falls
at the end. As Augustine one day said to his friends:

> Nobody can make yesterday come back; tomorrow is already
> treading on the heels of today, pushing to "get it over with." We
> should be more concerned about living a good life in our pre-
> sent "now" so that we can get to those wide open eternal spaces
> where we will not need to worry about "getting over with" any-
> thing.
>
> *Sermon 124,* 4

Sometimes we are tempted to ignore the reality described
by Augustine's words. Our hearts become sticky like a hum-
mingbird's tongue. We flit about in our present trying to find
sweet nourishment, something to love and call our own.
Finding such a lovely thing, some blossoming twig or other, we
reach out to grasp it, hoping that it will hold us in place so that
we can enjoy the delight of the present forever, trying to ignore
the persistent pull of the current of time that calls us to move

on. This is not to say that it is terribly wrong to sometimes take time off in our sail through life to enjoy a particular pleasant moment. Even the strongest ship must "lay to" every once in a while to take on supplies and get its bearings. The danger comes when we spend too long clutching our delightful twigs, refusing to move forward with our lives.

It is truly sad when this happens because the vitality, indeed the *beauty,* of a human life depends on its movement. There is nothing so ugly as a person who never grows up or a sixty year old who tries to act like an adolescent. A human life is not meant to be a one note affair; it is meant to be a song. To have a melodic song every note must be sounded at its proper time and then passed on so that the next note can make its contribution. The beauty of the whole comes from the coming and going of each individual moment of sound. So too the beauty of an individual's history comes from each moment of life occurring at its proper place and then disappearing forever into memory (*Confessions,* 11.28). A person who tries to strike all the notes together creates cacophony. A person who tries to hold onto one note too long is sadly boring.

Since our movement into the future is inevitable, how much better would it be for us to let go of our past and present, to stop fighting the current, and plunge towards our destiny with a laugh? But to do so we must be literally converted, turned around from the comforting "now" so that our attention is no longer captured, and our hearts are no longer "stuck" to the pleasant twigs and blossoms of our present.

It is the only reasonable thing to do. We cannot stop our progress towards the Great Falls, which are the edge of eternity, by grasping at the good things of the present moment. They are no more lasting than we are. The twigs that we so desperately clasp for security, our wealth or our career or indeed even our loves, are not planted on some unmoving shore. They are in the midst of the stream with us. In the words of Augustine: "They are smoke and wind and they flow past us like a river rushing towards the sea" (*Commentary on the Gospel of John,* 10.6.2).

Holding on to them, we move downstream just as fast as before; the only difference is that now we move along together.

We must be prepared to turn from both the good and bad
in our present. Only then can we accept ourselves for what we
truly are, little vessels floating temporarily on the stream of
time until the day when, in accordance with God's providential plan, we shall plunge over the Great Falls into a hidden
place we cannot even imagine.

Faith tells us that there is "something" on the other side of
our time here. Even in nature streams do not disappear once
they plunge over a waterfall. Rather, they begin a new peaceful
life of gentle movement into the endless ocean beyond. And so
it shall be for us, once we let go of the twigs that are holding
us in place. The current of our time is rushing past. It is time
for us to join it and see what world waits for us beyond the
crashing cataracts and rising mists ahead.

River Blindness   11

What a great gift is given when a doctor comes to a blind person and cures his blindness! What reward can be given for such
a remarkable cure? You may say "Well, give the doctor piles of
gold!" But the doctor gave you *sight!* To be able to see is worth
more than any amount of gold. What, then, can we give to the
divine doctor who so heals our earth-dimmed eyes that we are
able to see even the colors of eternity?

Commentary on Psalm 26/2, 8

As we travel down the river of our lives, we would like to
know for certain where we are going, but on most days we
seem to float through a dark mist. We would like to better
understand the people who travel along with us, but they seem

hidden from us. We would like at least to understand ourselves, but this too is made difficult by the mystery of our true "self" and our pretending to be something other than what we are. We are carried along by the current of time and we are blind.

The story of Jesus' curing of the man blind from birth (Mark 10:46-52) can perhaps help us face our own disability, can give us hope that our blindness can be cured too. Like the blind man, we were born with weakened sight, unable to see our destiny or the necessary means to achieve it. It is as though we come into existence with cataracts on our souls, doomed to live grayly in a world of brilliant colors. We are blind to the truth of our eternal lives, unable to see the God of the world in which we live (*Commentary on Psalm 9*, 23).

Even in mundane things we depend more on the words of others than on our own experience. They tell us what the world of our future can be like; they give us hope that we can achieve the good things that they promise, but which we have yet to see.

Thus, when we were children we were told "Eat your dinner!" and "Take a nap!" so that we could grow big and strong, but we did not know for sure that any of this would happen. When we were little we could not understand what it might be like to be truly big and strong.

Later on, when we were teenagers, we were told that if we were faithful to our schoolwork, we would become smart and people would look up to us as someone who was very important, but we could not know for sure that this would happen. As a teen it was sometimes hard to imagine how it would be to feel important.

When we were young adults we were told by our friends that someday we would find a true love, but we did not know for sure that this could happen, nor how we would feel when it did. No one can understand or feel the ecstasy of love until they actually experience it.

In the prime of our life we were told that we could have a grand old age, and we put away funds to prepare for it, but we could not be sure that we would retire gracefully and we did not know how we would feel with nothing to do, and every day to do it.

Finally, if we are lucky, at the end of our life someone will come and promise that some day we shall be well again and that death will never threaten us again. We truly will want to believe it, but again we cannot *see* it. We have no experience of what a life without sickness or death will be like. Once again we must live out our last days on this river of time buoyed up by hope, a hope based on one who has seen our future and who assures us that it will indeed happen.

As long as we live this side of death we will be like the man born blind, but like him we can anticipate a cure by truly *wanting* to see, by *hoping* that one day we will see, by never giving up *trying* to see. He indeed is a worthy model. After a life lived in darkness, being pushed here and there by those who could supposedly see, being supported by the pity of others, he never gave up hope that one day he would be able to see the world as it is.

One day his hope became reality. Jesus came to him and he opened his eyes, and for the first time in his life he saw! And, wonders of wonders, he was able to see much more than the road and the crowds and the trees and the human Jesus standing before him. He was able to see Jesus-*God* and in that vision he was able to comprehend the world for what it was, a place where God lived. He was able to see his destiny and know that the Jesus who had cured him was the one certain way to that goal. If he had seen only the human Jesus, he perhaps would have said "Thank you!" and gone on about his business. But once he saw Jesus-*God,* the vision compelled him to rise up from his stagnant present and follow Jesus into his future. He was blind no longer and was able to happily put aside all memories of his blindness and, now *seeing,* to follow Jesus down the road that led to the land beyond all times, the eternal city where the sun always shines and *everyone* can see.

Just now we are on the way to that land of perfect vision but it would be comforting to see a bit better just now, to see who is there to lead us through the rest of life. Augustine believed that such improved vision is possible. As he said to his people:

> Just as we have never seen Jesus as he was on earth, so we now cannot see him as he is now, waiting for us in heaven. But if you believe in him, you are truly seeing him. You say "I can't see him standing in front of my eyes!" but the reason for this is quite simple. You can't see him standing *before* you because he is now living *in* you, in your very heart.
>
> *Sermon 263, 3*

The Need for Love 12

> Each person is as his love is. Is it earth that you love? You become earth. Is it God that you love? Shall I say that you will become God? I would not dare to say this on my own but listen to God speaking through Sacred Scripture: "I have said that you are gods and children of the Most High." (Ps 81.6)
>
> *Commentary on the First Epistle of John, 2.14.5*

Every sensible person knows that we cannot control the ongoing flow of the river that carries our lives into the future. Like it or not, we grow old in body, if not in spirit, and sooner or later the body collapses. We get a leak in our boat which can no longer be offset by dedicated baling. However we *can* control what happens next, whether we will plunge over the Great Falls of our death into the quiet pools of heaven or into the dark abyss where God is absent.

Now, as we float along through our days in that vessel of solitude that is our life, we hear an insistent voice. It is the voice of our hidden God entreating us, commanding us: "You *must* love! You *must* love everyone and everything! You *must* love those who love you and, indeed, even those who hate you!"

The first reason for this need to love is that it makes this life bearable. We do not feel so terribly alone when we carry another human being in our heart. We do not feel so terribly unimportant when we know that we are carried in the heart of someone else. But there is a deeper and more important reason for our need to love. By our effort to love, by at least *trying* to love, we exercise that power which alone can unite us with God. As Augustine says: "If you begin to love you become more perfect. Have you begun to love? Then God has begun to dwell in you" (*Commentary on the First Epistle of John,* 8.12).

His argument for this divine indwelling is firmly grounded in Scripture (Rom 5.5), which declares that the only reason why we are *able* to love in any noble way (that is, in a way where we think more of someone else than we do of ourselves) is because the Spirit of God has taken up residence in us. With this divinely given power of love we are now able to have some say in the eternal direction of our lives. We come to understand the proclamation of Augustine: "My love is my weight; by it I am carried wheresoever I go" (*Confessions,* 13.9.10). It is only through our love for others that we are drawn out of that dank, dark prison of solitary self, and truly begin to *live*. Loving nothing, we remain (as Augustine says) "lifeless, detestable, miserable" (*Commentary on Psalm 31,* 2.5).

Our love is not confining but liberating. Drawn by it we are forced to lift up our eyes from the depths of our little boat and reach out to the world beyond. Far from trying to capture our loves in our own narrow space, we leap out of our lives to become one with theirs. We are drawn beyond ourselves to embrace all the lovely things around us. And, though we may not realize it at the time, in going out to others in love we are stretching to embrace divinity. Indeed, if we love properly the things of this world and especially the people who share our journey through life, we inevitably set our course towards that one who is the source of loved ones, the cause of our existence, that one who has made us creatures that *must* love if we are to find happiness.

But we must love properly. We must love the things in this world as they are, true goods but secondary goods, goods that will not be forever. In this life our loves seem always to be conflicting and at times unrealistic. We love our things as though they will never corrupt; we love our human loves as though they will never die. It is hard not to. The things of this world are lovable and are present before us each day. God is lovelier than all of these, but is not as evident. One who is married wakes each morning with the vision of their lovely spouse, not the vision of God. One who has a beautiful place by the ocean sees each day the beauty of the earth, and only by reflection sees the beauty of God in the colors of the sky and sweet smells of the sea that make the quiet dawn glorious. To love the present good things of this world takes little effort; to love a God somewhat hidden now and to be revealed only in our future is more difficult. But this must be done if our river journey is to end in happiness. We must reach out in desire to the divine even now if we are to strengthen that "gravity" in our lives that will insure that we shall fall into the arms of our Eternal Beloved at the end of our time.

Just now that future is uncertain. We cannot be sure that in the end we shall fly to God on the wings of our love. Even though we are drawn by nature to do precisely this, that pull of gravity must be accepted by our desire. It is still possible that this will happen. Even if we seem to be terminally addicted to loving the things and people of time, it does not have to be so. There are no steel chains holding us to this earth. If we are trapped by earthly things, it is only by our desire for them; and, through the grace of God, it is always possible to break such "spirit-chains" that stand in the way of our rising to the heavens (*Sermon 344*, 1).

We need to love, then, because it is only by loving that we can break out of the prison of self. It is only by loving that we can even now be drawn into the heavens. It is only by loving now that we can insure that we will love and be loved eternally on the other side of the Great Falls of death.

But it will never be easy. One can understand why, when the young Augustine was trying to break the chains of his desire for the goods of earth, he prayed the following prayer:

> O God, hear me as I tremble in this darkness and reach out your strong hand to me. Hold your light before me and call me back from my wandering so that, with you guiding me, I may return again to myself and to you.
>
> *Soliloquies,* 2.6.9

It was a prayer for nothing else than the grace to love well.

Partners   **13**

> In the act of loving we dwell in our lover with our heart.
> *Commentary on the Gospel of John,* 2.11.2

It is lonely floating on a river by yourself, especially when the river is your life. We are told in the book of Genesis that this solitariness was the way it was at the beginning of the human race. As the story goes, God created the first human being, a man, and then apparently went about other business. After a while he returned and saw that something more needed to be done. The man needed a companion. God had created other living things, the plants of the meadow and the birds of the air and the animals of the land and the fish in the seas, and presented them to the man to ease his loneliness. The man was very smart (we men have since deteriorated greatly) and when he looked at all these living creatures he understood them so well that he was able to give each a name, a name that captured their very essence. The man truly appreciated the beauty and the vitality of these living creatures, but still he was lonely. Some of them would make affectionate pets, but none seemed likely to be a good partner through the times ahead. The dogs did not seem to understand what was going on, and the cats did not seem to care.

And so God made another creature, one who was equal to the man in being the best reflection of the divinity in all creation, but one who was at the same time wonderfully different. God created the first woman, forming her body from the body of the man to signify the intimate bond between woman and man, and creating her soul directly to signify the intimate bond between woman and God.

Then God said to the man:

> Here is one with whom you can share your love; here is one with whom you can *become* one in spirit and in body. I have made you alike so that you can be true partners, helping and enjoying each other as you float through your lives. Your lives will remain different, but you will be bound together as no other beings in creation. I command you to love each other and help each other and put up with each other. I command you to cure each other's loneliness with your love. And if children should result from your union, I charge you to give them a good beginning on their own river trip, showing by your example what it means to be in love, showing by your love that it is possible for a human never to be alone in time or in eternity.

And so it has been ever after that, as each human being begins to journey in their solitary boat down the river of life, they are granted the power to love, the possibility of finding another who will join them as a partner in love, to make of their lifeboat a loveboat. Finding a love, our loneliness disappears. Our loved ones can bring happiness even to our most somber moments, and they make our moments of joy into an ecstasy that is a preview of heaven itself.

Before our loved one joins us we live with the hope that there is *someone* out there on the broad expanse of the river of time who is just *meant* for us, one who is destined to become *one* with us someday. And after they leave us in death, they still live in our memory, and even in the midst of our sadness we say with amazement: "For a time this beloved was *mine!* For a time there was a lovely human that I loved more than myself and (wonder of wonders) who seemed to love me too!" Our human love keeps us company as we continue to search for the God of love. In loving a lovely human being, we discover hope.

No wonder we celebrate our marriages with such joy. At our marriages we take time off in the midst of our rushing times to celebrate the faith and hope and love of two human beings who say to each other:

> The world indeed is passing and nothing seems secure, but at least our *love* will be forever, our *love* will never cease. We, like the rest of the human race, are plunging down the swift short river of this life, but now we move *together*, hand in hand, through its violent rapids and placid pools. No matter what the future holds in store, we shall face it *together* because we are bound together by a bond stronger than our rushing times. We are joined now by a bond that will last even till the end of time . . . and continue even beyond.

On the day of their wedding, lovers pray that their love will bind them together through all the time that is given to them. They pray that if it must happen (as it sometimes does) that one must go before the other into the eternal sea, that their love will bridge even that great chasm. The one who has gone before will carry their love with them; the one left behind will carry their love deep in their hearts until that eternal day when they shall be once again united in heaven.

And what will their heaven be like? It will be a place where finally and forever they will be at peace and still, with no more rushing about, no more twisting and turning through violent waters. It will be a heaven where they will finally and forever be at home with the ones that have indeed loved them more than the rest: that human being who was their faithful partner in life; that great Lord of Life, who saw in their love a reflection of his own love for all humankind, Jesus Christ the Lord.

Separation from a Loved One   **14**

> The death of a true love can never leave us free from grief if their companionship during this life was our support and our joy. There are some who say that humans should not grieve when they lose a loved one. Well, if they want to ban such grief, let them command that all human love be emptied of every tender feeling. If it is impossible to do this, so too is it impossible for us not to suffer bitter grief when a loved one dies, a loved one who gave so much sweetness to our life.
>
> *The City of God*, 19.8

A recent news item reported that the police in New Orleans found a seven year old boy roaming the streets at midnight. When they brought him to the station, the social worker on duty asked him, "What were you looking for?" His response was, "I was looking for someone to hold me."

The little boy's wish is a reasonable request for any human being. To float down the river of our life is difficult enough without having to do it alone. We all need to find someone to tie up with, someone who will bring their lives close to ours so that we can continue our journey together. As Augustine once remarked, "When you care about someone and they care for you, each drop of time becomes precious" (*Confessions*, 11.2).

When we find someone to love who seems to love us, we can become so excited that we dearly wish that the person would give up the little vessel that defines his or her life and come join us in ours, to fulfill the dream of young married love, to become indeed "two in one." But we must know that this is impossible and, indeed, if we think about it seriously, it is not even desirable. We should not want to consume our loves, nor should we want them to consume us. Love is a bond between *two* humans, not a melding into one. What we love in our lover is their distinct loveliness, their separateness that fills out our gaps, their special loving care that accepts us for what we are.

Augustine remarked once that we are lucky if we can find even one such loving friendship in our lifetime, but indeed we need more than one. For some of us the journey down the river is long, and it seems to be in the nature of things that our life span will see a series of meetings with and separations from different loves. Even if we find that one great love of our life, the number of years of sharing love together will always be problematic. It depends on two lives, ours and theirs, and either can end without warning. More often than not, those who deeply love meet death at different times. Never separated in life they are finally separated at death.

Death is not the only cause for the separations of this life. By their very nature most human relationships are transitory. We want friends and we need friends, but we have no way to control their ebb and flow in our lives. We all share the same river of time and we are all going in the same direction, but the whirls and eddies of the currents drive us off into different directions. Children grow up and make lives of their own. Though they may, and most of the time do, continue to love their parents, contacts can become infrequent. Old friends are separated by distance and after a while we have difficulty remembering them at all. Where once we were a high priority in their lives, we become quasi-forgotten, a name at the very end of the Christmas card list, a phone number which now must be checked through information.

Such ordinary "separations" in the midst of life can be painful if one of the former "lovers" still holds the other deep in their heart. To pine for a former love is not unusual, but it makes no sense to agonize forever. It is better by far to let them go and concentrate on the past good times shared, giving thanks for the blessing that allowed the currents of our lives to bring us together for even a brief moment. Of course sometimes the separations have no long-term dramatic effects. We miss them, to be sure, but when perchance we meet them again, we discover that our lives have moved on. We still look at each other with affection, but then get on with our lives, happy that our love has found happiness with someone else.

The most wrenching separation in this life occurs when a love who has been with us both spiritually and physically for most of our trip through time leaves us in death. We humans love passionately, and sometimes unreasonably so. As Augustine once wrote (thinking of how he felt when a friend died):

> Like every human being whose soul is tied in knots by loving things that cannot last and by grief when they are lost, I lived in misery. . . . How crazy it is to love a human being as something more than human!
>
> *Confessions,* 4. 6 & 7

Such unreasonable love is indeed crazy, but this is sometimes the way we love our loves; we love them as though they will never be separated from us. When we do love in this way and our loved one dies, it becomes difficult to continue with life. I know of one man who, when he buried his beloved wife of 42 years, effectively died at the same time, though he was buried some years later. Physically he remained very much alive, but his spirit's longing carried it beyond the Great Falls and it was no longer interested in the pedestrian functions of "staying alive in time." Appetite disappeared, sleep became sporadic, and each day was spent in a numbness that came close to being a living death.

It is a shame when this happens, but it is understandable. Even though faith tells us that our love is happy in a better life, even though saints like Augustine tell us that our loved one still loves us from beyond the Falls, that we are not alone because Christ lives in our heart, that someday we shall see our love again in a land where there are no separations, still we are sad. We want to *see* them, *hear* their voice, *feel* their touch! Our grief is not eased by a promise that we *will* see them; we want to have them here *right now*.

If we are lucky, union with other loving friends will help us get through our separation. Like Augustine after the loss of his friend, we find that the kindness of rediscovered friends or friends newly found will help us realize that we are not alone even though we have lost our great love to death. We still miss our love, but now at least we can wait in patience till we meet and love again.

Early Leaving   15

> A parent fears that their child will die before them. A husband or wife fears that their beloved spouse will die first. Can God make all their wishes come true? All we can do is believe that he knows the best order for his creatures to live and die.
>
> *Sermon 296, 5.6*

Augustine's analogy for life as a river flowing towards a distant eternity is often helpful for understanding our present condition, but it can lead to a false expectation, the expectation that our eternity is somehow far away. We promise ourselves and those we love many years before death, and when this does not happen, we feel that we have suffered a catastrophe beyond comprehension. When the one who dies is our child, we feel that this death is especially unfair.

Perhaps another analogy for human life is more helpful in such truly tragic situations. It was suggested to me by my memories of happy summer days sitting in the calm shallows off Miami Beach, my body lapped by the warm azure waters, my head barely above the surface, my eyes looking across the sea towards the seemingly limitless horizon. As I moved about, my splashing created small bubbles on the surface, which momentarily floated like individual capsules of rainbows, eventually disappearing into the great expanse of the sea. As I sat enjoying the experience, I thought to myself:

> If only I could rise above my life and look down upon it from a great height. Would I not see that my life in time is nothing more than a tiny bubble floating in an immense sea, that the line between time and eternity is only a thin membrane easily pierced, that it is only a delicate bubble-surface that separates my narrow life now from a infinite life beyond?

In this picture of the human condition, what we call "death" becomes merely a movement through the thin membrane from life to life, from our present tiny bit of life to a life without limits.

It is a fact of our life in time that we are never that far from eternity. From our first moment of existence in our mother's womb we are surrounded by, supported by, buried in, almost crushed by the immensity of the eternal sea. Once we have passed into the next life, if we were to look back, we would no doubt wonder why we had been so fanatically attached to the narrow, confined life that we lived in this bubble of time. Just now we are very much attached to our "bubble" and understandably so. It is the only life we know. Like a fetus comfortable in the dank darkness of the womb, we cannot imagine what an independent life in the light might be like, and if ever offered the option to leave or stay, we might say to our savior, "I will stay where I am, thank you very much!"

Of course, staying in place is impossible. Eventually we must be delivered from the body of our mother, just as someday we must be delivered from the body of our time. To return to Augustine's river analogy, we cannot stay on this plateau forever. We can accept the inevitability of this fact with some equanimity as long as we do not feel that we have been "cheated" out of this life, that we have had a fair chance to make our mark, to fall in love, to have some fun.

This feeling of "deserving" a reasonably long portion of earthly life is the reason why we are so disturbed when a child dies. It seems that the poor thing was never given a chance at earthly joys. It is especially hard to accept "early leavings" when the death seems to make no sense, when it comes from a random, accidental event or from a cruel human attack. In some ways, death from a childhood disease is easier to accept than death from random violence or human malice. To die of disease or decrepitude is part of the human condition. For a child to die by murder signifies something terribly wrong in the universe, the presence of an evil that seems satanic.

Augustine, who lost his own young son to disease, was perhaps still trying to make sense of his loss when he wrote to a confrere:

> When someone asks why souls are created for those who are going to die so young, the only response that can be made is that we must leave such matters in the hands of God. We know that the things that occur in time are planned by his love and that this includes the moment when a person is conceived and the moment when a person dies. If God counts the leaves on the trees and determines their formation and their fall, is it likely that he is indifferent to the appropriate span (sometimes short, sometimes long) for each human life? Is it not likely that he would make certain that no life is shortened or lengthened beyond that span required for it to sound its proper note and thus take its place in the harmony of creation's song?
>
> *Letter 166*, 5.13

It is a fact of human existence that some will leave for eternity from a life barely begun, while others will depart much later, carrying with them the good and bad residue of a long life courageously but imperfectly lived. We all share a nature that demands we change and grow as long as we live, but the length of that growth is different for every one of us. There is no good time or bad time to die for any of us; there is only our time. We do not know when that time will come. All that we *do* know is that death comes in its own good time, that time which is indeed good because it is determined for each of us by the providence of God, that God who is above us and before us and, indeed, with us as we race down our separate ways to the time and place where we will plunge into eternity.

Jesus came to break the barrier between this passing life and a good life in eternity. Walking this earth he was indeed "free among the dead" because death had no power over him (*Sermon 231,* 2). Perhaps that is how we should think about our dead, especially our dead children. They are not "free among the dead" so much as "free among the living," freed, finally, from the limits of the tiny bubble of life in which we all spend our time now.

Alone on the River   **16**

In this life all of us are travelers so covered with flesh that our hearts cannot be seen. In our journey we carry our own heart and each heart is closed off from every other.
Commentary on Psalm 55, 9

In this and other passages Augustine hints at one of his greatest fears, indeed the greatest fear of every human being: the fear of being alone on the river of life, the fear of being alone when the time comes to face the Great Falls of death. It is truly a sad, fearful prospect, to live and die alone. It can be nothing but a life of tears. As Augustine once remarked, "It is not easy to laugh when you are alone" (*Confessions,* 2.9.17).

To avoid *not being alone* is a difficult task because it is much, much more than simply never being by yourself. You can go through life surrounded by people but be very much alone; you can live by yourself and yet not be alone. Being alone is not the same thing as solitude. Solitude is a positive state chosen by an individual who seeks some relief from the hurly-burly of life in order to think more intensely about God and human loves, to pray to God and for the human race, to sit quietly waiting for God to speak. Those who are truly alone in this life are not so because no one else is there; they are alone because they realize that no one cares about them.

The anxiety that we feel facing the prospect of being alone as we continue our journey through this life comes from the fact that we are made to be intimately related to others, God first and then our human loves. As the words of Genesis (2:18) testify and our experience confirms: "It is not good for a human being to be alone." At the same time, because we are humans with a hidden "inner self," we are destined to spend many of our days as solitaries, beings destined to be born alone and die alone even when surrounded by crowds, beings destined to live through much of their lives in a core of solitariness that no one else can touch.

That we should have such an inner silent hidden core is not a weakness. It is our most important perfection, a center in which we are able sometimes to hear God speaking, that throbbing internal furnace that is the source of our power to love, the place from which our burning love for others responds to their perceived love for us.

Our feeling of aloneness comes at those times when it seems that we are loved by no one, when we listen for the voice of God and hear nothing. It is at such times that we understand the cry of Christ at the hour of his death: "Why have you forsaken me?" When he voiced those terrible words he was not physically alone. A few of his friends were close by at the foot of the cross. His words were thus not a call for company; rather they reflect the "aloneness," the dark despair, that can tempt the human spirit when it seems that there is no one who can help us through the bad days of life. They reflect the terror that can consume a human soul when it seems that even God has departed.

The cure for "aloneness" is difficult to achieve because it depends on finding a friend, and true friendship is not easy to find. Part of the reason is because it involves more than a caring for the other; it demands knowledge of the other's heart, some sort of awareness of the other's hidden center, what they are really like, what they really think, what they truly love. It demands at least enough knowledge to create a trust whereby we feel free to pour out our innermost thoughts and feelings, knowing that they will be received with understanding and sympathy (*83 Various Questions,* 71.5-6).

The friendship that will cure human "aloneness" is thus far different from what today television and movies call a "meaningful relationship." As described in the modern parlance, this mostly temporary "mating" seems egocentric. The relationship must "do it" for me, satisfy my needs, or be discarded. True friendship is quite different. It is a union of hearts whereby there is no longer a "me and you," but only an "us."

The problem with having such human friendships is that they must be reciprocal, and at some stages of life it can happen that there is simply no one who knows us well enough to care about us as a friend. It is possible to outlive our friends and lovers. It is possible that our condition in life makes us not only homeless but also friendless. At such times the only cure for human aloneness is to know that we have at least one friend, the God who put us here.

But to cure our "aloneness" we need more than simple knowledge. Faith is a great gift but it does not necessarily make us feel better. It does not prevent us from having an occasional "dark night of the soul." To have a human love at a distance, one who truly loves us and tells us so from time to time, does not take away the sadness of separation. To escape aloneness we need to have them *here* with us, to *feel* their love for us, to be able to *hold them close* to us as we return their love.

In the same way, belief in God will not cure our aloneness; only the feeling of the presence of such a friendly God will work. Christ's terrible cry on the cross demonstrates that the feeling of "not being forsaken" can sometimes escape us. All that can be done then is to wait patiently for the despair to pass. And pass it will because in good times and bad, the river of our life rolls on. Our life will inevitably pass through the Great Falls of death into the light-filled world beyond, a world where we will have a true union of hearts with all those who loved us in life, and the God who loves us in time and eternity.

In the meantime it is a great gift to have a truly loving, lovely human friend. They can help us through the dark stretches of river when even God feels far away. They may not be able to cure the sickness or anxiety or hurt that tortures us, but at least in the midst of our bad time we can feel that we are not alone. And that is truly a wonderful blessing.

Full Boats and Empty Hearts   **17**

We must be content to have no more than we need as we journey through this life. Why accumulate so many extra things when the course is so short and "stuff" only makes the travel more difficult?

Sermon 167, 3

There are many things we can do wrong as we float down the river of life in our tiny boats. There is only one overriding thing that we must do right. Whatever happens to us, we must commit our lives to the hand of God. We must carry him in our hearts, or at least hold our hearts open to him.

There are many ways we can prevent God from coming into our lives. One of them is by accumulating too much "stuff." We float through life and see ourselves surrounded by so many beautiful toys that we just *must* have. Slowly but surely we begin to fill up our tiny boat with "stuff." We say:

> Well, I really need "stuff" to live on this river. I need to gather stuff for lunch today and to provide for lunch in the years ahead. After all, I don't know exactly how long I will be floating along here. I must provide for my future.

   Such reasoning makes good sense. As I sit here with my heaviness pressing down on my spirit (and even more on my chair), it is evident that I am no angel. I must provide for my bodily needs. If I do not, this majestic vessel of God that is "me" will soon corrupt and disappear. But it does not make sense to accumulate more "stuff" than I need; it makes even less sense to allow myself to be driven by a passion to get as much "stuff" as possible. As I rush about trying to increase the value of my portfolio, Augustine laughs and says to me:

> You are always upset; you are putting things in storage; you are racking your brain trying to figure ways of getting more. In the daytime you are upset by doing business; at night you are haunted by fear. Why are you doing all this? For yourself? For your children? How absurd it is to rush about gathering so much unnecessary "stuff" for those who will someday die!
>
> *Sermon 60, 3*

   This human passion for things seems to flow from our nature, perhaps as an aspect of our drive for self-preservation, perhaps from a false conviction that we must have "stuff" for our lives to mean something, perhaps from the insane conviction that more "stuff" will make us lovable. God knows there are many humans (perhaps most) who do not have much stuff, but this does not preserve them from the passion. As Augustine noted long ago, it is hardly a sign of virtue to have nothing but to desire everything. Rich or poor, the passion for possessions can consume the mind and eat up time.

The greed of the rich, those who seem to have everything and yet want even more, is especially hard to understand. Their boats are already filled, but they pile in more and more. Like Noah in the ark, they want two of everything in their little boat, making room for only one jackass . . . themselves. It is so silly. They are on the same river as the disadvantaged and all make the same sort of splash on the other side of the Great Falls.

The tragedy of one living with a passion for things is that they will tumble into eternity with full boats and empty hearts. From miserliness they will come to misery. At the moment of death their boats will be filled with perishable objects, but their hearts will be empty because their passion for "stuff" left no room in their hearts for love. Their earthly loves took second place to their material goods and gradually died out of lack of nourishment. Their love for the divine never developed because somehow the God who made them seemed less real than the pretty things they had made for themselves. Like the young man in Mark's Gospel (10:17-30) who was held back from following Jesus because of his riches, these sad souls may have otherwise been good people, but their "stuff" took priority over the call of God.

The story of the widow's mite (Mark 12: 41-44) gives a happier picture of how one can successfully navigate through this world of beautiful things. It also teaches this important lesson about life on the water: "The one with the lightest boat will have the easiest journey." The reason why this is so is obvious. If we fill up our lives with lots of created things, we will have no room for the presence of God. Furthermore when our boat is weighed down with "stuff," it becomes hard to keep from being swamped by passing events.

Such worries do not plague us if it is God who fills our lives. If someone wants to come and take part of our God, that is fine. There is plenty to go around. With God we are not weighed down, we are lifted up. We seem to skip over the waters of this life into our future. Best of all, we will never be alone no matter how long our journey lasts. Surrounded by our "stuff," we may say that we have found love; but the only love discovered is our own passion for things, things which cannot love us back. On the other hand, when we love God more than our things, we love someone who not only loves us, but who also can give us the grace to delight in loving him also.

All things considered, the poor widow who gave her little offering in the temple had a successful journey through life. It was sad that she had lost her husband and apparently had no one to care about her. It was unfortunate that she had barely enough "stuff" to get by. But, at the same time, she was filled with God, the only wealth that can be carried over the Falls into eternity.

It is a shame that all of us cannot be like her. It is a shame that sometimes we still overload our little boats with so many things, because neither our little earthy life-vessels nor the "stuff" they contain can last through the Great Falls. In eternity our hearts will be empty and our "stuff" will be gone.

Blowing Bubbles   **18**

> All the glories of this world that humans spend their lives seeking are enjoyed as in a dream. If they do not wake up now when the waking can be helpful to them, they will be roused involuntarily on a day not of their choosing when it will be too late. Then they will discover that all those temporal things that they had considered important were but a dream and that the dream has passed away.
>
> *Commentary on Psalm 131*, 8

The constant challenge of living in this world is to recognize our life for what it is and to deal with it accordingly, to recognize what is truly important and to concentrate on these important truths at the proper times. This is what Jesus was trying to tell the Sadducees a few days before his death. Here they were spending their life arguing about the theology of resurrection, and all the time they should have seen the clear message of their scripture that "God is not the god of the dead, but of the living. All humans are alive in him" (Luke 20:38). As they continued their own journey down the river of time towards eternity, Jesus was saying to them:

> Stop wasting your time sitting on the deck of your boat blowing bubbles! Look around and see where you are going. Listen to what I have revealed to you and know that you are going to live forever and that you had better live now with that fact in mind.

There is nothing wrong with taking a few days off in our busy lives to blow some bubbles, to have some time for doing something childish or silly or, indeed, something that is nothing at all. I, for one, had a grand time as a child sitting on a Jersey beach blowing bubbles. I had one of those little pipes obtained from that treasure house of childhood riches, Woolworths. With a correct mixture of soapy water and remembering to blow out rather than suck in (a procedure I learned in a painfully empirical way), I was able to blow beautiful, shimmering bubbles that would float to the sky capturing all of the colors of the rainbow. I was terribly proud of my bubbles. They were pretty and round and pulsated almost as though they were alive. Most importantly, they were MINE, a creation of ME, a reflection of all that was good in ME, a sign that indeed I was superior (as my mother insisted) to all those other kids who could do nothing more than dig holes in the sand. I was indeed the bubble-master of Wildwood, New Jersey.

My sadness came when I realized that my one claim to fame was transitory. Even without interference, my bubbles would soon disappear. There would be a "pop" and they would be gone, leaving nothing but a drop of memory on the sand. I too was changing. Very soon I reached an age and size where sitting on the sand blowing bubbles was no longer viewed by others as being worthy of praise; it had moved from being cute to being odd. The lesson was clear. A short spell of blowing bubbles is fine in its proper place; it only becomes dangerous when one dedicates a life to it and takes seriously the evanescent creations that quickly pass away.

The various bubbles that we create in later life have the same goal as my childhood seashore bubbles: to make something that will set us apart, to make others look up to us, perhaps even to make them love us. Augustine is speaking about blowing such bubbles when he tells about the farmer whose passion is for more and more land, the soldier who seeks power by having others fear him, the lawyer who places his hope for glory in his power to manipulate words and be a part in a "noble profession," and the merchant who seeks wealth in foreign trade (*Commentary on Psalm 136*, 2-3).

Augustine describes all these ventures as "a dedication of one's life to a river in Babylon," a river which, like every bubble, is quickly passing away. His point is not that being a farmer, a soldier, a lawyer, or a merchant is evil in itself. There is nothing wrong with farming the earth, or soldiering for the community, or making a bit of money, or even spending one's life dealing with words. (Augustine himself practiced that trade.) But it is wrong to make such evanescent activities the most important thing in life.

When we put too much of ourselves into these passing activities, we become like children chasing disappearing bubbles on a sandy beach, unaware of the beginning sunset that will summon us off to sleep. In our sleep we may dream of our day of "pretty bubbles," but the nature of our sleep, whether it be peaceful or disturbed, will be determined by how "humanly" we lived the glorious day that was given to us, a day which had a time for blowing bubbles, but more importantly had a time for loving the humans around us and praising the God above us.

The Search for Glory   **19**

> If the glory of the world makes a lot of noise, it is because it is
> the roar of water falling on rocks. See how the water dashes
> along, how it glides away and disappears. Take care lest it drag
> you with it.
>
> *Commentary on Psalm 136, 3*

The story of Jesus during the last week of his life teaches
an important lesson about this moving river that is our life. It
is simply this: the distance between glory and crucifixion can
be very short. Even so, most of us would not mind having a
little glory in our pedestrian lives. As we plod through our
ordinary days we say to ourselves things like the following:

> I wish someone would appreciate me. I wish someone would
> give a party where the banner behind the podium testifies to
> what a fine person *I* am. I wish someone would volunteer to
> write my biography for the edification of others. And if all this
> is impossible, I wish at very least that my kids would pay at-
> tention to me.

We don't like to admit it, but this thirst for glory is part of
human nature. How else to explain our worship of passing
celebrities, those who are applauded for doing things different
from the run-of-the-mill existence of most of us? How else to
explain creating a show on the lives of the "Rich and Famous"
for those of us who are the "Not-Rich and Uninteresting?"
How else to explain our passion for being on T.V. ourselves,
even if it is only by running in front of a camera reporting a
neighborhood car accident?

We wish that someone would celebrate our keeping the
faith rather than throwing a party for those who gave up their
promised dedication for the sake of greener pastures. We wish
that more would be made of our perfect attendance at school,

rather than celebrating those party animals who eschew any such boring life-styles. We wish that someone would say "Good job!" to us when we stay faithful to the same spouse for a lifetime, rather than reporting in avid detail the continuing saga of the constantly changing relationships of the so-called "beautiful people." Does our stability make us one of the ugly people? And why spend so much effort on a fitting retirement party for us (where the condemned employee eats her/his last meal before redundancy) when no one thought to celebrate us during our active days so often sweat-filled and anxiety-ridden? Retirement parties can be nice, but even the best of them seems to be more a celebration of our "passing" than our "being."

Yet that is the way that the glory of this world seems to work. People pay attention mostly to those who are different. Even Jesus attracted little attention when he was simply a teacher; he made the papers only when he began his miraculous healing, perhaps because bringing people back to life has always been more interesting than boring them to death. He *really* attracted attention when he got into politics, critiquing the religious and civil status quo. For that they not only paid attention to him; they killed him. True, if he had stayed in the anonymity of his ordinary life, he would never have had his Palm Sunday; but also he would never have suffered crucifixion.

There is a chance that sometime in our life we will be given a moment of glory, our own private Palm Sunday when we are the center of adoring, cheering attention. On such grand days people will listen to us and learn from us or, at very least, enjoy us. These are days when we will seem to have something to say to the cheering crowds, or to *be* something for them that will make an important difference in their lives. If such times come to us, we may make our own the jubilant words of the prophet Isaiah: "The Lord God has given me a well-trained tongue, that I might know how to speak to the weary a word that will rouse them" (50:4).

However, if we are sensible (remembering perhaps that we and they are on a moving river), in the midst of this palm-waving adoration, we will keep our ears open so that we can hear the Lord deep inside us warning:

> This will not last. Your Palm Sunday, your day of glory, will not last long. For a while on this rushing river you may be surrounded by worshipping crowds, but then you and they will move on. You will become passé in the passing of time to all but those few who truly love you, who loved you when you were only lovable to them, who will love you still when the rest of the world forgets you.

If only we can hear the Lord's warning about the passing of our "palmy" days, we will be prepared for what comes next: perhaps persecution, at least anonymity. In some ways the first is better than the second for one who is still frantically seeking recognition. Persecution has a bit of perverse glory attached to it. At least when you are strung out on the rack you are the center of *somebody's* attention. But persecution does not normally follow glory; anonymity does. Most who for a moment are called to glory are not thereafter invited to "give their backs to be beaten" (to use Isaiah's phrase). Instead they must face the retreating backs of the formerly cheering multitudes who have moved away in search of a celebrity who is new and more interesting.

If we can face such indifference bravely and with good humor, then we will have indeed learned how to live without glory on this ever-changing river that is our life. As we float along in our anonymity it will perhaps be helpful to remember that at the end of *his* life Christ was surrounded more by the indifferent than by persecutors. The crowds on Calvary came to see the show, not to throw stones at him. It is also instructive to remember that for Christ there were only *four* days between adulation and indifference, and only *five* days between the palms and the cross.

Finally we should remember that, like so many other aspects of our nature, the desire for glory is not bad in itself. Indeed, one could argue that our desire to be a constant center of attention, our wish to be *eternally* glorified, is the very force that drives us towards heaven. There our desire for glory will be satisfied because we will know that we are loved beyond all comprehension by an infinite God, an honor that certainly we will not deserve, but will enjoy anyway.

A Friendly Take-Over   **20**

> Do you think that people who have reached the age of thirty are on the way up? Far from it! Once they reach thirty humans are already on the track that leads to true old age.
>
> *Commentary on the Gospel of John,* 14.4.3

To be thirty and to be told that you are "over the hill" is a depressing experience. Most of us do not like to admit that we are on the downhill slope of even our physical life at that age, though in fact we are. To be only thirty and to have others passing us on the jogging track is bad enough; to have them already passing us on the road of life can truly dampen one's spirit.

This truth was brought home to me during my first college teaching experience. I was thirty, a newly minted PhD, and thought myself in the prime of life. I still rushed the net in tennis (though more sedately than when I was seventeen), could play a game of basketball without dying, and thought that all in all I cut a fine figure of a man. Though I dressed conservatively (as befitted my position as a priest-teacher), I considered myself fashionable. I did not avoid looking in mirrors, as I do now. All in all I felt pretty good about myself. Therefore, I was not surprised when one of the boys in the dorm asked to borrow my suit for a party. I could see why he wanted to imitate the dignified fashion statement that I made every day for the benefit of a dazzled campus. It was only sometime later that I discovered that he was going to a Halloween costume party.

It is painful to discover at thirty that you are already out of the mainstream, that life has moved past without so much as a "hail and farewell!" At least when you are old you can say to yourself "Well! I have had my day in the sun, and in my prime I could have beaten out all of these who now replace me. At least I am respected for my past!" When you are passed over at thirty you cannot indulge in even that meager consolation. People are not respecting your past day of glory; they are judging that your day of glory will never come. To lose a job at thirty means to have to explain for the rest of your life why you were passed over, and the first answer that jumps to the mind of the questioner is that your best was none too good.

Indeed, to be passed over at thirty is a hard thing to bear with good cheer, but it is possible. The story of John the Baptist proves that. It is my belief that the most significant sign of John's virtue was not his early asceticism in the desert nor his powerful preaching to the hordes who came to hear him when he was at the peak of the career. His sanctity was shown most clearly when he was in prison, ignored and powerless, waiting for his destiny to be determined by the will of a corrupt and weak king. He knew that he would never get out of that prison. Indeed, soon he would be executed because of a king's drunken promise to a daughter who did an exotic dance at one of his parties. He was so impressed by her immodest gyrations that he cried: "I will give you anything you want!" Prompted by her mother, the king's mistress, the girl asked for the head of John.

What an end for this man who had been the most famous preacher of Israel! He was like a person caught in a corporate take-over, losing his job while still in the prime of life, told by the world, "We no longer have use for you! Get lost! You have already become invisible to us!"

John was like the thousands (millions?) of elderly living out their last years alone in retirement villages and nursing homes, separated from their children, ignored by their old friends. A lesser person than John would perhaps have felt the sadness of one who dreamed of being the savior of the world, only to discover that someone else had taken up the task. All that such discarded prophets can do is to watch and wait for that last great event in their lives, their death.

John was caught in a take-over, a friendly take-over, but a take-over none the less. His job was finished; Jesus would continue his work. Christ had come and now (as John described it) "I must decrease and he must increase." The one thing left for him to accomplish was to find a place for his old friends. His followers may have had hopes that one day John would get out of prison and resume his career (he was after all only in his early thirties), but John knew better. He was a dying planet and it was important for his friends to attach themselves to a rising star, a star that could brighten their remaining days on earth, and eventually show them the way to heaven.

And so John sent his friends to visit with Jesus. They came back filled with excitement, reporting that he was preaching to large crowds, that he was forgiving sins, that he was even raising the dead. If John had not been so saintly, he could very well have felt a twinge of jealousy. He had never been able to perform such wonders and the crowds were already forgetting that he had ever existed. If John had been less virtuous, he may have indulged in the sad reverie that sometimes infects the elderly, in the midst of a pedestrian present, reminding bored listeners of the glorious past.

But this John did not do. He let go of his times of importance and waited for the Lord to come to him in death, however it might come. It came to him wrapped in absurdity. John did not realize even that most minimal human dream, the dream of dying with a bit of dignity. Instead, his head was unceremoniously and secretly cut off because of a king who got drunk at a party, a jealous mother, and a lascivious adolescent. Jesus called him the greatest born of humankind, and perhaps the reason why he was greatest was because he had the virtue to wait patiently for the coming of the Lord as the rest of the world sped by into new times, times that had no further need for a thirty year old man named John.

Good and Evil 21

Here are examples of people who will in the end be saved. They are those who, with faith in Christ, are moved by his love to perform whatever good works they do but who are far from perfect. They will often get angry with others but still are ready to forgive when asked. They are perhaps too attached to what they own but still will give some of their wealth to the poor. In this life God loves them for their good acts and gives forgiveness for their evil, and in the next life they will join the ranks of those who will reign with Christ forever.

Against Two Letters of the Pelagians, 3.5.14

At some moment in our lives, most of us ask questions about the evil and good that we find in this world. Both are equally great mysteries, but usually it is the evil that we speak about the most. Why is there so much evil in this world that God created? Why is it that children must die of AIDS? Why are there innocent victims of human cruelty? Why is it that millions starve in the midst of plenty? Why is there so much viciousness in the human species? Why must life be destroyed by natural disasters: floods, earthquakes, and violent storms? Why do things go bad in a world that was made by a good God?

We ask "Why evil?" but the existence of human good is sometimes an even greater mystery. How can you explain the heroism of humans in the midst of difficult conditions? How can you explain a sick child patiently bearing its pain? How can you explain a young man who sacrifices his life to save his sister? How can you explain the silent horde of truly GOOD people, people who are just and kind and brave even under the worst of conditions?

Of course, we do not raise questions about good and evil in the universe right away. Children seem to assume that good rules the world; it takes a cruel or uncaring adult to convince them of the opposite. We do not raise the question about good and evil until we are well along our journey on the river of life, and usually it occurs when we witness the good things or bad things that are happening in the boats of others. When evil is close to us, we do not question it; we suffer it. When we experience the ecstasy of a great good, we do not ponder it; we enjoy it.

We raise the questions of "Why Evil? Why Good?" when they occur at a distance, when we see a stranger perform a truly heroic act, when we come to realize that a silent saint lives just next door, when we hear of a cold-hearted killer who takes life with no more feeling than when ordering coffee. In such situations good and evil are almost tangible. They are too real to be denied; they are too extraordinary not to demand some explanation.

The explanations are always less than satisfying. The answer to the question "Why evil?" may be eminently reasonable but it is hardly ever consoling. Thus, it does not give much comfort to a person who has just lost all of their possessions in a terrible fire, to repeat to them the words Augustine wrote long ago in the quiet of his monastery: "It makes no sense to seek to blame someone when things are as they ought to be. It is foolish to complain when things of time pass away" (*On Freedom of the Will*, 3.15). What he says is certainly true. There is nothing terribly unnatural about things of this world coming and going or humans dying. But repeating such facts of life will not take away the despair of someone who has lost all that they had worked for or, worse still, has lost a loved one, to whom they had given their heart.

Augustine himself was not as amazed about the evil in the world as he was about how much good was there. Evil was understandable once you realized (as he did through personal experience) that the little boats in which we float through life have holes in their hulls, and through them all kinds of strange ideas and desires enter. As he put it to members of his own religious community: "Everyone promises themselves that they will live a good life but they have been put into a furnace and have come out cracked" (*Commentary on Psalm 99*, 11).

Because we move through life in a boat that is cracked, there is always the danger that we will be swamped and sunk by grave spiritual catastrophes like murder or adultery or blasphemy. But we can also be sunk by the accumulation of small perversities that slip through the cracks in our life like sea water slips through the faulty seams of an old boat. To live a good life we must therefore not only be looking out for death-dealing stormy passions; we must also bail out from our lives the tiny drops of perversity that we choose to indulge in each day (*Sermon 77b*, 7).

Augustine was convinced that we need the grace of God to avoid doing any evil act, and without that grace any of us (himself included) had the potential of repeating any crime recorded in human history, and even of creating some new ones that had never been seen before (*City of God*, 22.22). We need help to do the good, and we need it every day of our lives. One injection of God's grace will not heal our cracks forever. To use Augustine's homey analogy: "When you baptize a drunk, all you get is a baptized drunk. The sin is certainly forgiven but the habit remains" (*Sermon 151*, 4-5).

The only grace that is a final protection is the grace of perseverance, and you can only be sure that you have received such grace at the moment you die in God's good graces. Augustine himself spent the last three days of his life reciting the penitential psalms that he had painted on the walls of his room. He was very, very weak, but he realized that he still had the time and energy to reject God one more time.

We shall always live in an imperfect world and the living will never be easy, whether the times are good or bad. As Augustine told his people, the constant challenge for all human beings is to control themselves and to endure (*Sermon 38,* 1.1). We must control ourselves when enjoying the good times and endure when in the midst of the bad. We must fight the temptation to despair when things are going badly; when things are going well, we must fight the temptation to depend on the good lasting. Both bad days and good days will pass and we must be ready to face the new day coming, be it bad or good.

Finally, we must be humble enough to realize that even though we strive to be saintly, we will never be perfect. The protection against despairing of ourselves comes when we are realistic enough to realize that we are called to *become* saints and are not expected to be saints right now. With the help of the grace of God we can someday be saints, but just now we must always be ready to say to God "I'm sorry" and start again trying to be as perfect as we can be in this sometimes crazy, mixed-up world.

The Rainbow of Hope 22

> The Son of God became a human being and thereby experienced all that we humans go through. So let us live in hope and recognize how great we are in the eyes of God. Who can despair because they are human when God himself became a human?
>
> *The Christian Combat,* 11.12

In his commentary on the Gospel of John (33.8.1-5), Augustine suggests that there are only two insurmountable obstacles to our salvation: false hope and despair. Through despair we believe that we cannot do good; through false hope we believe doing good does not matter. We say to ourselves, "The gentle good God is infinitely merciful. I can do anything my little heart (or great lust or overweening ambition or dominating pride) desires and I will be forgiven." Like a child of permissive parents, we get the idea in our head that whatever we do will be just fine because we (the beloved child, the cute kid) have done it. We end up even sillier than our silly elders, not realizing that if nothing we do matters it can only be because *we* don't matter, that the ultimate disrespect of a human being comes in not taking them seriously.

I suspect that throughout human history despair has been more common than such false hope. The most powerful temptation on this sometimes dark and turbulent river of life is the temptation to simply give up fighting the tides, to let events take us where they will. Such despair can attack even the most fervent believer. Indeed, it is nothing less than the "dark night of the soul" described by the great mystics. It is not that the despairing believer does not take God seriously; rather they take themselves *too* seriously. They say "My sins are just too big; I am just too worthless." They think that their evil actions are too evil for even an infinite good to erase; that their lowliness is too abject for even an omnipotent power to lift up.

Scripture tells us that there was a time when humanity justifiably had no hope. They had been wounded by sin. Their wings had been clipped by bad decisions and heaven was beyond their reach. Humans plunged faster and faster through the trials and troubles of this life to the sound of the roaring Great Falls in their future, a Falls that promised not a better life beyond but only an eternity of hunger, where they would be far removed from all that they wanted most, peace and love and a feeling of being a success. In such a state not only were humans unable to cope; they had no hope.

But then everything changed. As humans fell deeper into the dark waters of despair, a light began to shine. Suddenly a rainbow appeared in the gray mists rising from their rushing lives. God came to humans in the person of Jesus Christ and promised them a land of light, a land where they could be happy, a land where no longer would they be tossed about, a land where humans would not perish but flourish.

The story of Noah (Gen 7-9) prefigured this return of hope to the human race. Unfortunately we often miss the hopeful conclusion of the story. We think more of the destructive flood that threatened to end all of creation rather than the rainbow that promised a glorious future ahead. In sending the rainbow God promised Noah and us:

> Never again need you be afraid for your eternal lives; never again need you fear that there will be no chance for you. I give you this sign of my promise. When the storms rage over the waters of your life and the clouds gather bringing ominous darkness, I will create a rainbow against that darkness to remind you that the storm will soon be over. As you raise your eyes from the threatening waters of your times and see the colors of the rainbow against the dark sky, be reminded that I have promised that I will not destroy you, that I will never leave you alone, that a better life awaits you on the other side of the Great Falls. As you see the brilliant colors spanning the sometimes darkness of your life, you will remember that there is a land of light that is coming, a land of the yet unseen Son who even now showers a bit of his brilliance across the shadows of passing storms. When you see the rainbow, remember that I have promised to save you. And as you come closer to that Great Falls that marks the end of your travels, you will see that death is nothing more than a journey through rainbows, the rainbows that sparkle in the mists rising from the Great Falls ahead.

It was the promise of Noah's rainbow, and even more the promises of Jesus Christ, that inspired Augustine, in the midst of his turbulent life, to say to his God:

> I look forward to my eternal goal even though I am still torn this way and that by the turbulent changing currents of my life.

But now I know that this will end when I become purified and then softened by the fire of your love, able finally to be fused into union with you forever.

Confessions, 11.29

Finding God in Creation   **23**

In my mind's eye I imagined the whole of your creation as a vast mass made up of different kinds of things and I pictured you, O Lord, as encompassing this mass on all sides and penetrating it in every part. It was as though there were a boundless sea and somewhere within it a sponge filled through and through with the water from this infinite sea. This was the way I pictured creation to be, filled everywhere and to its very depths with the divine presence.

Confessions, 7.5.7

This vision of God containing the universe and flooding each and every one of its parts was Augustine's way of describing the relationship between God and creation. Though he never again uses this analogy of sea and sponge (perhaps because of its materialistic flavor), the image of God "containing" creation (as an infinite sea contains a finite sponge) and "being contained" by it (as a sponge everywhere absorbs and is soaked by the wetness of the immersing sea) can be found repeated again and again throughout his writings.

Creation was called from nothingness by the power of God and thereafter necessarily "rests" in him, depending on him for its continuing existence. God embraces it and is absorbed into its every pore, completely and wholly present as much in its least part as in its totality. God truly fills heaven and earth just as an infinite sea would fill every crevice in a sponge immersed in it. It is because of this divine presence that:

the stars move in their courses, the winds blow now this way and now that, deep pools seethe with tumbling waterfalls shadowed by mists, meadows come to life as their seeds put forth the grass, and animals are born and live their lives according to their proper instincts.

A Literal Commentary on Genesis, 5.20.41

Thus, if humans want to discover traces of the divine, all they need to do is open their eyes and turn to the book of creation. There, on every page, they will find a nature flooded with the presence of God (*Sermon 68,* 6).

This is so because the universe is more than just filled with God; it reflects God. In a real sense we can say that when we look at nature, we see God. All of creation has God as its model. No one would begin to build a house without first having a plan, an idea of what should be done based on the perfections of what has been done. Before creation took place, the only perfections that existed were in God and, therefore, God could not create without having his creation reflect himself in some way. Of course the analogy between creating a universe and building a house breaks down once the house is finished. The builder can walk away with no damage done; but if God were to leave creation, it would cease to exist (*A Literal Commentary on Genesis,* 4.12.22). Rather than God being far distant from creation, it can be truly said that he is more deeply embedded in it than is its most inward part (*Confessions,* 3.6.11).

This being the case, it is not a waste of time to look at the wonders of the universe outside of us, to sit on the deck of our boat, smell the air, and watch the passing clouds. We are not thereby turning away from God; we are gazing upon an aspect of his order, his beauty, his goodness. Augustine says to us:

Just think of the world in which we live! There is an infinitely changing beauty in the sky and the land and the sea. What varieties of color do we see in the changing moon and sun and stars! There are the soft shadows of forests at noon, the shades and smells of spring flowers, the different songs and exotic plumage of the birds. And how amazing are the animals that surround us, the smallest, the ant, even more amazing than the huge whale. Think of the grand spectacle of the sea as it vests itself in its different colors, sometimes green, sometimes purple, sometimes the bluest of blue. And how grand it is when there is a storm, especially when we are not forced to sail on its heaving surface but can watch it safe and warm on the shore, gently caressed by its mist.

City of God, 22.24

I believe that Augustine would even agree that sometimes sitting on a bench high above a shining sea can give us a more powerful feeling of God's presence than kneeling in the dank depths of a dark cathedral. The sea is God's creation; the church is built by human beings.

We are born as sensual creatures appreciative of the sounds and smells of the world around us; only later do we learn with some difficulty the pleasures of the spirit. It is for this reason that, though the discovery of God must end in the inner "self," for most of us it begins in the world outside (*Commentary on Psalm 145,* 5.). Just as the experience of human love frequently comes before the experience of loving God, so we rejoice in the beauty of the everyday world before we come to reflect on the beauty of a God who could bring such beauties into existence. Augustine's advice to the person seeking God is to begin by looking at the surrounding world.

Ask the lovely earth and the lovely sea, ask the lovely breeze and the lovely heavens, ask the orderly march of the stars, ask the sun making the day gleam with its beams, ask the moon moderating the darkness of the night with its gentle glow, ask the living things which move through the waters and those that wander on land and fly through the air, ask your own hidden soul and your visible body . . . ask any of these wonderful creatures and hear them answer: "Indeed, it is true; we *are* lovely. See how lovely we are!" By their very loveliness all these humble creatures point to their God. Who but "Loveliness Himself" could make even these passing things be so lovely?

Sermon 241, 2.2

River Nights   **24**

God gave us the night so that we might rest from our daytime rushing about. And then he created the stars to shine upon earth and bring light to our humble dwellings. He did not want us to live in absolute darkness and he did not want the night to be without its own beauty. He gave us the gentle light of the night because he knew that we could not bear to live always in the glare of the blazing sun.

A Literal Commentary On Genesis, 2.13.27

Our time on the river is a combination of day and night, and it is good that it is so. It is hard to live in a day without a sunset or a night that goes on forever. Indeed, much of the beauty that we enjoy on this ever-changing river is in day following night and night succeeding day.

Although once we are beyond the Great Falls of death we will rejoice in endless day (constantly in the presence of the Son), just now we could not stand such brightness. We need our times of sunny activity but we also need our nights of restful shade. We can neither work all the time, nor should we be in a state of permanent rest. Like self-winding watches we need activity to keep ourselves going. Like our friends the plants we need the night to restore energy. Augustine knew this better than most. As a busy man (sometimes too busy) he used his daylight hours productively. As an insomniac, he treasured the quiet nights when he was able to get a little sleep. Perhaps this is the reason why, as an old man, he looked forward to his death. "Finally," he thought, "I will be able to get some true rest!"

There is perhaps another reason why we treasure the night in this life; in the evening quiet it is easier to recognize God. Perhaps that is the reason why Jesus was born at night. At night the shepherds could see the heavenly host and hear the singing. During the day they would have been blinded by the sun and distracted by the bleating of their daytime charges. The fact that they were able to see God in a poor infant proved the principle that would later guide the three wise men in their travels: "When searching for God, it is better to do one's traveling at night."

We need the day to do our work but it would be hard to live always in such unremitting glare. The sun would quickly blind us to the expanse of the universe around us and in us. We need nighttime shade to see where we are going, to find traces of God in our passing world. Only in the soft light of twilight or midnight moon or beginning dawn can we see the starlight of God twinkling deep inside our spirit. Then God shines on us as softly as the moon, painting the sometime mists of our lives a delicate lavender, softening the sharp edges of the troublesome crags that clutter our days. At night we can see the moon and remember that it reflects a hidden sun, that it promises a new day coming, a *good* day whose rosy hues can even now be glimpsed just beyond the horizon.

It is a great gift to be able to have restful nights, to sleep and then wake in the quiet dark:

> to see the stars glittering in the immensity that is the universe, that universe that is held like a child's toy in the hand of God . . . to see the earth softly glowing in the moonlight . . . to lift our eyes to the shining moon and know that a new day will soon be dawning.

And then to sleep again, now filled with excitement at the prospect of the coming dawn.

Long ago Jesus came to earth at night so that he might lead us to that dawn. He has promised that when that dawn comes we shall awaken to a day without end, a day without the need of a night because never again will we need restful sleep. In the light of that everlasting day we will not need darkness to find our God. Then we shall stand face to face with him in the light.

Letting Go 25

> Hope urges us to look to the future. Stretch out your hope to future things as yet unseen! Don't look back! Ignore the noisy world, chattering away behind your back, trying to make you turn around and turn away from what Christ has promised, trying to make you seek your happiness in things you can never retrieve, things that are gone forever!
>
> *Sermon 105, 7*

We spend much of our lives in letting go of the past, and often we do it voluntarily and happily, especially when we are still young. For example, I myself looked forward to that moment when I could let go of childhood and leave behind those short pants which my mother insisted I wear as her *baby* (though at the time I was shaving and over six feet tall). And it was a great relief when I finally left school behind and began to learn something. And I was deeply happy when I left behind my state of unemployment to take up the noble profession of philosopher, a great career where few know what you are doing but many consider you wise because they cannot understand a word you are saying. In all these cases my letting go of the past was not traumatic at all. Indeed, it was embraced as a necessary step towards a new and vibrant life, new work, new loves, new experiences.

It is not so easy to let go when you are old, but it is just as necessary, indeed more necessary, since there is little time left to make many mistakes. When the call to let go comes at the end of our river experience it can be a truly wrenching event because in most cases it is not something that *we* choose. Rather it is chosen for us by others, or simply by the circumstances of the time. It is painful because we are not letting go; we are let go.

This happens when, after many years practicing an honored profession, or at least having a good job or (at very least) an occupation that gave us some reason to get up in the morning, we discover that we have become redundant. Our work is retrenched and we find that we are not a part of the new trench; we are part of the dirty pile of detritus on the side. To add insult to injury, the reasons for our demise seem almost inconsequential. Perhaps *someone* has decided that there was a need for young blood in our position, someone with a fresh outlook, someone with a view on life not hampered by lessons from experience. Or perhaps we got sick and when we recover we find that our place has been taken by another, creating the impression that for so many years we have only been filling a slot, taking up space, providing a function that could be performed by anyone or (if the job is phased out) by no one at all.

Being retrenched is bad enough, but it is even worse when we are simply buried in the existing trench. We are given nothing to do. We are allowed to stay on the job but there is a clear impression given that we are superfluous, a museum piece kept around as a cause of wonder for visiting children. We lunch alone because we are out of the loop. We put in time and are encouraged to take time off with the implication that we will not be missed.

Or perhaps worst of all, the need to let go is not suggested by others. It is a need that we feel growing deep inside our heart, a feeling that despite the smiles of those around us we have indeed "lost it." We realize (but do not admit) that no longer do we have the fire or fervor to do our old work effectively. Perhaps a friend will recommend time off for regrouping and retreading, but we know that such a device will not work. One cannot regroup a dissolving life, and retreading works only when the tire is basically sound. But we are not. The air has gone out of our enthusiasm. We say to ourselves, "I really *should* retire," but then an inner voice asks, "But to what?" When one is old and approaching the end of the river there is no easy answer to that question.

We might say, "Well, if I retire I will have more time for my old loved ones, for my old friends!" and this is a good solution if we have not reached a period in life where these too must be let go. The need for letting go that comes with age can involve the letting go of loves. What can we do but let go when a beloved wife or husband dies? And sometimes we must even let go of living loves. Parents cannot continue parenting children forever. At some point children must be allowed to make their own way in the world. To try to hold onto adult offspring is destructive and unrealistic. It is even more destructive when one not only tries to hold onto them, but even tries to continue giving unwanted advice on how to run their lives. As Augustine observes, it is natural for parents to caress their babies and rejoice in their innocent return of love, but good parents do not want their babies to stay that way forever. They look forward to their beloved infants letting go of infancy and moving forward to a new stage of life (*Commentary on Psalm 127,* 15).

Sometimes old friends must be let go too. When we have been separated by large blocks of time and space, it becomes impossible to recover the intimacy of old. They have moved on, perhaps found new soul-mates as the center of their lives. Meeting them anew after long separation, your affection for them is still present but you become shy about expressing it as you did in the warm summers of your youth. Despite your desires, the past cannot be recaptured; it can only be remembered fondly, perhaps with quiet tears. It is too bad that this is so, and you naturally feel sad about it, but your sadness should not stand in the way of letting them go, being happy for the new happiness that they have found somewhere else with someone else.

As we move further and further down the river of our life, while remembering the good times past, we simply *must* bring some sort of closure to what is gone so that we can move towards what is to come. We have been promised that some day we will meet old loves again in a land where our memories can become reality once more. There we will be able to renew acquaintances with a purity and innocence impossible just now in this world of secret fears and hidden agendas. We certainly would not want our loves never to move on, and we should not want this for ourselves either.

We should look forward to our own letting go of the past so that we might be ready for what comes next. The process may even make us feel younger; it certainly is better than being sixty and trying to act thirty. That old skin that we are hanging onto, those past experiences and past dreams must be gotten rid of for new dreams and hopes to bloom. Augustine recommends that we follow the example of the snake in this. When it feels old and flaky (and who does not on some days), it sheds its old skin, revealing one that is new. We move constantly into the future and must not be trapped in the past by a suffocating nostalgia. Like the clever snake, "We must shed our past before we can rejoice in the new things that are coming" (*Sermon 64*, 6). We must not let our homesickness for the past stand in the way of our hope. No longer able to enjoy our youth, we must let it go if we are ever to be able to enjoy the beauty of the last stages of our life.

The Hospital Ship 26

If you have any doubt that humans have been wounded, just look at the troubles we have in life. How else to explain why we are so terribly dumb, so filled with crazy passions for vile

things? And how about our illnesses? No medical library can
list the innumerable ways in which we can be sick and often
the cure is worse than the disease!

City of God, 22.22.1-4

There is no doubt that Augustine, believing as he did in
the equality of human beings and their common goal, would
agree with the axiom that "We are all in the same boat." In
essential matters there is nothing to distinguish one human
being from another. We are all constantly in motion, riding the
waves of the river of our life towards the Great Falls at the end.
We all shall certainly die, and we all have the same chance of
reaching that eternal, infinite sea beyond the Falls that is the
place of God.

Indeed, we are all in the same boat and, Augustine would
add, it is something like a hospital ship. We are floating towards our destiny in a *cracked* condition, in a body that is
falling apart, with a spirit that sometimes cannot see where it
is going, and sometimes indulges in wild desires. Augustine
had a great feeling for the sick and distressed because he knew
from his own life what it was like. He almost died from fevers
twice in his youth, and he complained about ill health for most
of his remaining seventy-six years. Thus, when he came to list
the various maladies that torment humans, he was not speaking apart from his own experience. He knew how it felt to
have difficulty breathing, to have stomach problems, to have a
toothache. He knew how it felt to be confused, depressed,
exhausted.

He also knew that there was little we humans could do
about our various ills. It is just in the nature of things that on
some days we will barely manage to feel pretty good, and on
others we will feel downright rotten. These are hard times to
live through, times when we are physically ill or when we simply feel seasick, depressed and tired of our seemingly endless
trip through turbulent waters. We may put on a good front but
deep in our hearts we make our own the wail of Job:

Is not human life on earth a pain? Are we not all like slaves who long for the shade? Indeed, I have been given months of miserable days and troubled nights. If I go to bed I wonder if I will ever get up. My days come to an end without hope. They pass by whirling in the wind. I *know* that I shall never be happy again.

(7:1-4)

As we are tossed about in that poor broken boat that has become our life, we pray for relief. We pray that some savior will come to heal us or, at very least, we pray that our days on these troubled waters will come to an end. We may not be too sure of what awaits us on the other side of the Great Falls, but we hope that it just *has to be better* than this painful life.

We read the story of Jesus' cures and cry:

"Jesus, you cured Peter's mother-in-law; why not me?"
"Jesus, you cured the man born blind; why not me?"
"Jesus, you cured the lepers; why not me?"
"Jesus, you cured the people driven crazy by demons; why not me?"

But Jesus does not come and we feel even worse. Now as we sit in the little boat that is our life, we feel not simply sick but terribly, terribly alone. Friends try to help, saying: "I know just how you feel," but THEY DON'T! How could they? They are healthy and we are sick! Anyway, when we are sick we don't want sympathy; we want a HEALER! We pray to Jesus to come, but it seems that he does not. He is not there with a cure, and for us in our sickness that is the only proof of his presence.

In fact he is present, but we do not recognize him. He comes to us as a teacher, but we want a doctor. We want him to come as a miracle-worker, and he comes as a friend. It is instructive that when he had his first great day of healing at Capharnaum (Mark 1:29ff), he eventually had to escape so that he could preach. When he was in the midst of the frenzy caused by his cures, no one would listen to him. They did not want their doctor to make a lot of chitchat; they wanted him to *cure* them. But Jesus wanted to do more than cure them. He wanted to talk to them; whether they were healthy or sick was not important to him as long as they would listen.

And so too it is for us when we are in the midst of our illness. We may not get a quick cure but if we listen carefully, if we pay attention (and sometimes we are too sick to do even that), we can hear Jesus saying:

> I have come to be with you in your good times and in your bad. I have come to you to get you through this life, not to make every day a good day. I have come to help you see how these troublesome times are only part of the times of your life, that they are a bad patch on the way to an eternal sea where you will forever be well. And so, be brave. You are sick and I am sorry for that, but you are not alone. I am here with you.

River's End: Sea's Beginning **27**

> The power not to die that Jesus-God possessed was indeed great, but even greater was the mercy through which he freely chose to die for our sakes. He wished to die and come back to life again so that we might have hope that we could someday join him on the other side of death.
>
> *Sermon 362, 92*

As we move down this river surrounded by loved ones who come and go, we make our own the plea of the strangers who came to the disciples a few days before Jesus' death and said: "Sir, we would like to see Jesus!" (John 12:21). It is a wish that becomes stronger as we come closer and closer to the Great Falls that mark the end of our river life. In the distance we can see only the mist that marks the meeting of time's river with the eternal sea beyond. We would like to see that sea, to know where we are going, to know what and Who awaits us. But we cannot see; the mist rising from our death-falls is impenetrable just now.

Mostly those whom we have loved and who have disappeared into the mist never return. We believe that they are in a better place, in some eternal sea where they rest in the arms of God, but we cannot SEE them. We cannot SEE beyond the mist, and thus we live out our days in faith and hope, the virtues of those longing for a life that is not yet.

If we have lived life for any length of time, we have already lost many who have gone through that mist never to reappear. We miss them and cry out to the Lord, "Please, Sir, let me see my loved ones again!" But we cannot. The mist is too thick to penetrate, and our loved ones never come back to our river to visit. We dream about them, we see them in our imagination, but we can never touch them or hear them. They are beyond the mist and we don't KNOW what their life is like. We may believe that there is something beyond death, but we cannot SEE, and this we desperately want to do because it is only by seeing that we can truly know. Seeing is NOT believing; it makes believing unnecessary.

This is why that first Easter Sunday was truly an important event. It was the moment in history when a human being like us went beyond that mist, truly died and plunged over the Falls, and then returned to this river again. He did so to prove to his friends that there was indeed a fine place beyond the Falls, where every human being could live a perfect human life, body and soul.

Of course there had been an apparition or two like Moses and Elijah on the hill of transfiguration, and there had been some "bringing back to life," like the son of the widow of Naim or the return of Lazarus from the grave, but apparently these events did little to encourage the disciples, especially after they heard that Jesus had died on the cross. The apparitions that appeared when Jesus was transfigured were just that: merely apparitions, filmy visions hard to relate to one's own life. The resurrection of Lazarus came closer to home because it had (literally) more body to it. But it gave little evidence of what life on the other side of death would be like. Lazarus still ran into doors (rather than go through them as the resurrected Jesus did) and still seemed to need sleep and food. Moreover, it was clear that someday he would die again, going through all the pain and trepidation that such a wrenching experience entailed.

Indeed, it is entirely possible that, as the disciples hid in that upper room after Good Friday and before Easter, they may have cried out "Sir, we would like to see Jesus!" They, like us, passionately wanted to see someone who had gone through the mist of the death-falls and survived. Despite the fact that they had walked and talked with Jesus for three years, they had never seen him as he is and was to be for all eternity. They had all seen the human Jesus but, except for the vague reflection that three had experienced on Mt. Tabor, none of them had come close to seeing Jesus-GOD. More importantly, they had yet to see a *resurrected* Jesus, a flesh and blood Jesus who had gone through death and would never die again.

Easter speaks of a time and a place when a human went through the mist hiding the Great Falls of death, and then returned still covered with the dew of eternity. Indeed, since that human is also the Son of God, his promises about resurrection assure us that we have nothing to fear. He promised us that "Where I am; You also shall be" (John 12:26). By those words he promised that we too shall be resurrected; by his own resurrection he proved that ours is possible.

Augustine goes so far as to say that our future time in the grave is no more terrible than the past time we spent hidden in our mother's womb, waiting for the yet unknown life outside. Why then should we be so afraid? "Does it make sense to say that this God who is able to bring a fully developed human being from the womb is not able to bring a living human being out of a tomb?" (*Sermon 242A*, 2).

The River King   **28**

> The river of our times hurries us along, but like a tree sprung
> up beside the river is our Lord Jesus Christ. Do you seem to be
> rushing headlong down the stream towards an abyss? Hold
> onto the tree! Hold onto Christ! On these waters we are tossed
> about by the waves, but we have an anchor of hope already
> fixed in the land where Jesus dwells.
>
> *Commentary on the First Epistle of John,* 2.10

Augustine's image of a "roaring" and "rushing" river is an
apt image for the lives of most of us. Caught in the rapids, we
speed past our days and years as though they were standing
still on the distant shore. We can see them but they seem beyond our grasp. We whirl into our future impelled by forces
beyond our control and indeed beyond our ken.

It is no wonder that we seek something to hang onto,
something bigger than life that somehow gives our random
movements some purpose, some meaning. We seek a rule, and
even better, a *ruler* who will give direction to our existence:
something, someone, who is in control of our spinning life;
someone, something, to reach out to as we rush along.

As we plummet through life, each of us chooses *something*
to direct our lives, some goal to work for, some value to dominate our decisions. Some choose pleasure or comfort; others,
earthly success. There are some who will dedicate themselves
to the service of strangers, and others who will make their
families the most important thing in their lives. Some choose
a cause; some simply choose themselves. Even those who
choose nothing in fact choose something. Giving up on finding direction in their lives, they choose a randomness in which
every decision has the same value because none has any value.
Giving up hope, they choose despair. They take life as it comes
and do not search for any higher meaning, dealing with their

life by simply not thinking about it. Perhaps they seek oblivion through drugs or alcohol or trivial pursuits, making these instruments of forgetfulness the rulers of their lives.

Some gifted with Christian faith choose Jesus Christ as their king. They choose his values as their day by day guidelines. They choose his promises as the basis for their hope in the future. By a mystery of faith they come to believe that the Lord God actually said those wonderful words to the prophet Ezekiel, the words that console us poor sheep floating down this river of life:

> I myself will look after and tend my sheep. I will rescue them from every place where they were scattered when it was cloudy and dark. The lost I will seek out; the strays I will bring back; the injured I will bind up; the sick I will heal, shepherding them rightly.
>
> (34:11-17)

Unhappily, the fact that God cares about and rules the events of our lives does not mean that they will be free of tragedy. He promises only that there will be no final tragedy unless we choose it. He has promised, through his prophet Ezekiel (34:15-17), that at the end of the river of time he will destroy the "sleek and the strong," those who spent their lives believing that they were quite able to handle matters on their own, those who thought only of themselves and never of others. There will be judgment at the end of time, but it will be a judgment on what we freely chose to do with our lives.

In the meantime, with Christ as king of this river, we know that even the most turbulent life has meaning. It is watched by an infinite power who cares. With Christ as king of this river we have hope that when our end comes there will be something and someone waiting for us. There will be no surprises when that end comes because we shall find that the *something* is that which we have prepared for during our river days. We shall discover that the *someone* who waits for us is the very one we clutched during our earthly journey, the one who was with us from our beginning, even until our end.

Last Turn in the River   29

> What harm is there in a person dying when they by nature are destined to die? The real tragedy for dying persons comes not from their death but from the sort of life they have led. If they die healed by God's grace, then truly their death is not the sunset of a past life but a dawn of a new life that is infinitely better.
>
> *Letter 151, 7*

We make our way across this plateau that contains our time on earth with many twists and turns. Sometimes we come close to the brink of death but then turn away. It is not yet our time to die. We offer a sigh of relief saying, "Now I will appreciate the good things of this life even more." For a moment we forget that the limit of the broad plain on which we play out our earthly lives is never far away from us. Even knowing that some day we must plunge over the Great Falls at the edge, we spend most of our days convinced that we are moving in circles far from the edge of the plateau, that the danger of falling over is far distant, that each turning of our river's direction is always towards a new phase of life, not towards its ending.

As we circle and circle in the midst of our time of strength we may pretend that we will never die, but finally the day comes when we can fool ourselves no longer. Our lives seem to hesitate and then make an abrupt turn towards that time and place where God has predestined that we should enter eternity. Sometimes the change is clear and dramatic, like a clap of thunder that announces a fatal illness; sometimes the change is vague and ill-defined, like debilitating old age creeping over us like morning mist over a quiet marsh. In whatever way the change comes, we come face to face with the fact that the river of our life has made its final turning towards the edge, that we have experienced the event that will be the cause of our final fall into eternity.

It is important to recognize the turning, to learn how to live with it, to make it profitable for the eternity of life that is before us. Rightly accepted, it can bring a sort of freedom. We discover that we are finally free to let go. As we now move quickly towards the Falls there is no good reason to try to slow the pace. We change the focus of our lives. Events occurring on the plateau that we are soon to leave (the news of the day) become less important than the future rushing towards us, the unknown eternity beyond the Falls. We leave behind the crashing rapids of the plateau; we are free at last to flow quietly towards the brink. No longer is there work that simply *must* be done; there is only a diminishing life that must be lived nobly. We discover that there are no loved ones who absolutely *need* us, though they may think they do for a time. In any case, it is time for them to realize that their life must go on in time as the life of their dying loved one goes on in eternity.

No longer need we try to change the direction of our lives this way or that. Our direction is now fixed by powers beyond our control and we are free to go with the flow, not thrashing about but floating in peace, enjoying the scenery of the fast disappearing world. Assuming that we are not distracted by great pain or distress, we are able to see our time more clearly now. Our future is now set, and the opportunity to change the past has gone. All we can do is pray for a successful eternity, remember with joy the good times past, and say to God "I'm sorry for what in the past has been bad."

After spending a lifetime trying to be successful in life, there is a realization that there is no success or failure in its ending. Prince or pauper, saint or sinner, youngster or old fogy, the fall into eternity is the same for all. At the end one's success or failure will be measured only by one's desire for God and one's past honest effort to live a life on the plateau of time that was, all things considered, "not too bad."

When we come to this last turning in our lives, perhaps we can be helped by the example of Jesus. He was close to death many times in his life, but the final turn towards the Falls occurred about a month before his crucifixion. Then, in the little town of Ephraim some thirty miles north of Jerusalem, he took his apostles aside and said: "Behold, we are going up to Jerusalem where I shall die, but on the third day I will rise again" (Mark 10:32-34). Thus began his final turning towards the Great Falls.

The wondrous aspect of that last stage of his life was that there was no change at all in its character. He did not retreat into solitariness; he did not mope through his remaining days. Rather he walked firmly along his final journey, enjoying and using well each "now" left to him. He cured the blind in Jericho, went to a party in Bethany, led a parade into Jerusalem, and continued to teach in the Temple by telling stories to the folks who came to listen. He moderated arguments among his friends, and for the last time put his enemies in their place. Finally, at the very end he had a joyful private party with his mother and his closest friends.

How could he be so happy and productive in these last days before his death? The reason is simple. He knew that his human life did not end on Good Friday. He knew that when a human being plunges over the Falls, what awaits is not the tomb, but Easter resurrection. He could enjoy those last days on this plateau where human life rushes along, because he knew that Friday's death led to an even more vibrant Easter life.

He *knew* that this was his future; and he promised that so it would be for us. We too must some day go over the Falls, but now we know that there is someone on the other side who loves us so much that he freely chose to make the journey first so that he could show us the way.

Old Heroes   **30**

> My friends when you celebrate the great martyrs don't think
> that such a glorious end is impossible for you because no
> human persecutors are after you. Even today there is no lack of
> daily persecutions, whether it be from devilish temptations,
> your aching body, or simply the misery of a vexatious life.
>
> *Sermon 4, 37*

An old retired navy friend of mine who had survived
much vicious combat in the Pacific theater during World War
II would sometimes say (usually after a few drinks) that his
wish was that he would end his life at the ripe age of eighty-
four, being shot in the back by a jealous husband as he jumped
through a bedroom window. As it happened, he suffered a
stroke and spent his last months paralyzed in bed.

Of course, his dream was said in jest. He was a moral man
for whom adultery was unthinkable. But his jesting words re-
flected a serious hope, a hope shared by most of us, that when
our time comes to pass over the Great Falls of death, we will
do so still vigorous and in possession of all our faculties.
Unfortunately, as Augustine observed long ago, it is not in our
power to determine how our death will come. All we can do
now is to live so as not to need to fear our lives after death
(*Sermon 306, 2*).

Anyone who must face death is called to be a hero, one
who is challenged to confront bravely a frightening prospect.
There is a special heroism in one who deals nobly with a difficult death. Augustine suggests that one who says they do not
fear a painful death is probably already dead (*Sermon 348, 3*).
The patient endurance of the disabled elderly is truly worthy
of honor. My friend was perhaps more of a hero during his last
days of weakness than through all his years of combat. Unfortunately, no medals are given out in nursing homes. We

seem to be impressed only by extraordinary events and we honor only those who perform extraordinary actions, forgetting the ordinary miracles and ordinary heroes of daily life. We define a miracle as an event that is rare; we restrict the honor of "hero" to those who perform well in circumstances that are unique.

Thus, when we read about the early days of Christianity, we are impressed by the heroism of the great St. James, who in his early forties was the first apostolic martyr. At the same time we mostly ignore the bravery of his brother John who, like James, was once a "Son of Thunder," but spent the last half of his life in anonymity, caring for Mary until she died, and then being cared for and carried about by friends. There is a tradition that the old John spent his last years repeating himself (as we senior citizens are wont to do), saying over and over again: "Little children, love one another." History has recorded for all time the martyr James whose life ended with an act that was like a dramatic shout. It has pretty much ignored the old John who spent 100 years of life waiting for Jesus, finally ending his days with a whisper.

In like fashion, we make much of the good Dismas who offered his young life to Christ on Calvary, and we pass over the story of the old Anna and Simeon who, after living long and difficult years, spent their last days waiting for God. Their last days of waiting and doing nothing were not wasted because they were ready to recognize God when he was brought to them in the guise of a baby. They were the first to prophesy who this baby Jesus was and what would happen to them. And why were they the first? Perhaps because they were old and better able to see into eternity.

Who then are the ordinary heroes, the secret heroes of life? Are they not those in our own families who have survived with grace this life with its sometime disappointments and the sometime sickness and the sometime disability that comes with age, who have survived without losing faith and hope in God, and indeed with a certain amount of good humor?

I live in a monastery where most of our Augustinian sick and elderly are gathered. To be frank, I am somewhat frightened for myself when I witness THEIR disability (like the rest of humanity I ignore my own present peculiar disabilities). I witness their paralysis, their deafness, their sometimes calling out for no good reason, their patient silence in the midst of real pain, their sometimes lack of contact with anything real in THIS world (perhaps because the next is already more real), and (worst of all) their conscious living through day after day with nothing to do. Looking at them I see my possible future, a future that is hinted at by my weakening present.

At the same time, looking at such ordinary heroes who, now incapable of doing much that is considered "important" by this world, spend their days in prayer and reflection about the next, I am inspired by the lesson they teach. The lesson is that, with the grace of God, any of us can become ordinary heroes, waiting patiently for the coming of the Lord like Anna and Simeon, preaching quietly with our lives like the old John, as a diminished "Son of Thunder."

Scripture teaches that such ordinary heroics are not wasted effort in the eyes of God. The book of Revelation describes the end of time when, after the final judgment, long lines of humans (soul AND body now) will troop pass the welcoming angels into heaven. The old John (to whom the revelation is being made) asks his guide "Who ARE all these people?" And the answer comes back: "These are those who have *survived* the troubles of life" (Rev 7:14). This is what makes Anna and Simeon and John and the sick and the very old true heroes. Despite the troubles of life, they have *lasted*, they have stayed the course, still close to the God they now patiently wait for.

Hopefully someday I (and you) will be part of that troop of survivors. It would be nice if we did not have to go through sickness and disability to get there, but that we must leave up to the providence of God.

Caretakers at the Falls   **31**

> Nothing so proves friendship as bearing the burden of a friend.
> Take the example of deer. When deer swim across a river to an
> island in search of pasture, they line themselves up in such a
> way that the weight of their heads carried in the antlers is
> borne by another. The one behind, by extending its neck,
> places its head on the one in front. By bearing each other's bur-
> dens in succession, all of them are able to successfully navigate
> the raging river.
>
> *83 Diverse Questions,* 71.1

In ancient Greek mythology there was one demi-god who
was in control of the human passage through death. Charon
was his name and for an appropriate price he would ferry the
dead into the next life. If we are lucky, we too shall find a caretaker at the Falls, someone who will be with us as we prepare
to make our final journey.

For some of us, this caretaker (or better, "giver of care") will
be a family member who cares for us in our last days. For others it may be a caring nurse or doctor who becomes a surrogate
parent, helping us get through our birth into eternity, as our
natural parents brought us through birth into this life.
Sometimes it is someone who takes care of our spiritual needs,
praying for us and with us, performing the special rites of passage reserved for those at the edge of the Great Falls. At the
end our caretaker may just be a very good friend who comes to
visit, a friend who will talk to us or (sometimes more importantly) *listen* to us, a good friend who feels comfortable simply
sitting with us in silence, being with us as we make our way to
the end of our river.

Such caretakers are a great gift and should be appreciated.
It is truly rare to find someone at any stage of life whom we
can trust completely, friends who can be told *exactly* how we

feel. How many in life do we find to whom we can say: "I am completely, absolutely, irretrievably, immodestly, passionately in love with you?" More often than not we keep our passion to ourselves, lest we embarrass ourselves and the shocked objects of our fervor. How many people, when they enter our hospital room and ask "How do you feel?" will comfortably accept the answer "I feel rotten. I am despairing. I feel like I am dying and I am afraid"? More often than not we will just respond: "Oh, I'm doing pretty well!" and let it go at that.

To be a caretaker or care-receiver at the end of life is not easy. It is certainly not easy for someone who loves us to see us in the last stages of leaving them. It is not easy for one who has rejoiced in our beauty to see us in our ugliness, an ugliness more piercing because it is of the spirit. The truth must be told: the dying are sometimes a pain, even when we love them very much. It is hard enough to put up with a whining child; it is doubly hard to put up with a complaining adult who is acting like a child, who *knows* what they are doing, but who simply does not care. Using Augustine's deer analogy, it is like having the dependent "dear" constantly complaining about the quality of the support supplied by your increasingly tired rump.

It is understandable that there should be some complaining when someone is suddenly robbed of a vigorous life. It is especially hard when they have spent a lifetime being the "leader of the pack." After a lifetime supporting others, being a pillar of strength, and being the one with all the answers, it is terribly difficult to accept a time of life when we must depend on others to perform even the most humble bodily functions. It is humiliating, frustrating, and sometimes we are tempted to rail against the world, God, life, and especially those who are trying to take care of us. We are mad because we think we can do nothing, but in fact we are challenged to perform the most important function we can accomplish at the end of life: to be patient with our infirmity, to be kind to those who care for us, to try, even in the midst of our misery, not to make others more miserable. At very least we should thank

God that, though we indeed feel truly bad, there is another human being who seems to feel bad about our condition.

Many humans die without even that much consolation. What can be said to them? Perhaps only this: "If you must die without a human caretaker at the Falls, be assured that God will become your caretaker. He will sit and wait through your last hours with you." It is a great comfort when one can accept this truth of the Christian faith, for God is the most reliable and powerful caretaker of all. Even though we are surrounded by family, friends, clergy, doctors, and nurses, all they can do is be with us and hold our hand during our last moments in this life. They must stop at the brink. Only God can continue our journey with us. Only he can take care of us as we go over those Great Falls that are the door to the eternal sea beyond.

Setting Sun: Rising Light 32

> For those who at the end have been called by Christ, the delight in visible things is diminished. The inner self, now created anew by its passion for things invisible, turns away from the passing external light to that inner light which never fades. Illuminated by this increasing brilliance it seeks those eternal things that cannot be seen by the external eye.
>
> *83 Various Questions,* 64

It is a fact of this life that we are rushing down the river of our diminishing time towards the eternity that lies beyond the Great Falls. In such a tumbling state, as we speed past every present to an unseen future, as we run through every hour to a distant place beyond our experience, we long for some guidance that will help us live intelligently in the swirling waters. For us Christians much of that guidance comes from the words and stories enshrined in sacred Scripture. In truth, some of the messages are hidden in mystery; but others are very clear.

One of the clearest messages was given to the first Christians by Jesus Christ himself towards the end of his earthly life. Palm Sunday was over and Good Friday was fast approaching. He knew that he would soon be dead. Looking out over the excited crowd he also knew that some thought that death for them was far away. It was to such as these that he cried the warning: "Be alert! You cannot be sure when your end is coming!"

What Jesus was saying was that there is no sure sign when any of our lives will come to an end, when *our* time will come to plunge over the Great Falls that mark our death. Some, indeed, erupt in a foaming roar as they crash through the last violent rapids of life. But others slide gently towards their end, whirling in gentle pools and eddies up to the very brim of the Falls, then disappearing with nary a whisper of complaint into the eternal sea beyond.

It follows that no human can afford to live life today as though tomorrow were assured. We must enjoy and fully use today to perfect ourselves and bring joy to others because today is the only day that we certainly possess. For those too attached to this passing time, Jesus' warning can be a frightening message. But for those who see this river for what it truly is, a beautiful introduction to a life of beauty that is forever, the message can be great consolation. It says to young and old alike: "Whatever your age, whatever your stage in life, you are surrounded by eternity. The Lord is near and no one will have very long to wait before Jesus comes to take you home."

If we are convinced of this truth, we can face our end (whenever it comes) with equanimity. If we have lived a life of faith and hope and love, our last days can be like a soothing twilight. Our time is coming to an end and the setting sun is fast disappearing behind us as we fix our gaze on the Falls ahead. If we have been faithful, we are sometimes then given a great gift. We are not left in the darkness. The light outside us is indeed diminishing, all that seemed so bright and cheery on the river at noon, now quietly disappears into the lengthening shadows. But now a light begins to shine within. That same light that brought us into existence, that light that quietly gleamed unnoticed in the midst of the brilliance of noon on the river, now begins to dominate our lives.

The sun is indeed setting on our earthly lives but we are illuminated by a light from within. Like a night-light in the room of a child, it goes unnoticed in the brilliance of the day, but now as the darkness of evening deepens it begins to glow ever more brightly, finally illumining all that was so important to us in the light of day, softening the sharp edges of hurtful things, making shadows of those pleasant things that seemed so important when we were in the midst of our days. Now we can see the realities that are our comfort as we doze our way into eternity. These good things were always part of our lives but they were invisible, unseen because of the distractions of the glaring light and blaring sounds of the times. Now we can see them and know that we shall carry them into eternity with us: our memories of good things done and bad things repented; our realization that we are loved, that we are worth something, that we have lived a life that was not *completely* wasted; an awareness of a divine power that was and is with us and indeed *in* us through good times and bad.

It is this power that now shines ever more brightly in our soul. The sun that marked our time is indeed setting. But the Son, who will be with us through the death-falls and into the infinite sea beyond, is now rising ever more powerfully in our darkening days. The mists rising from the Great Falls ahead are in a shadow. But we are filled with a new light and we pray with Augustine: "O Lord, light of my heart, don"t let the darkness of life overcome me" (*Confessions*, 12.10).

Final Ending   **33**

> We love life, and we have no hesitation at all about loving life;
> nor can we in the least deny that we love life. So let us choose
> life, if we love life. Lead a good life now, and you will receive
> an even better one later.
>
> *Sermon 297, 8*

In our journey down the river of our life we are driven by
hungers; the hungers for life, meaning, and love. We want to
be alive. We want our lives to have some value. We want to be
loved by someone else. It is only when we approach our final
ending and reflect on what has gone before that we can see
that these hungers were there at every age, even though sometimes we did not recognize their presence.

In our first years on the river we did not think too much
about our hungers. If we were lucky, we were carried through
our early years embraced by others. We didn't bother philoso-
phizing about life. We just lived it. We did not worry about our
life having meaning; it was more important to find someone to
play with. We did not worry about being loved; we were satisfied by being fed and put to bed on time.

When we got a bit older our hungers became more appar-
ent, but still the hunger for life did not dominate our thoughts.
We were in the midst of our days of strength and seldom
thought about getting sick, much less dying. We were, however,
beginning to worry about the meaning of our lives and we spent
a fair amount of time searching for it. We also became concerned about finding someone who would love us as we sometimes thought we were, a gangling, stupid, unattractive nerd.

Later on, as we took on greater responsibilities, family and
work took up much of our time. We still had our hungers but
had little chance to think about them. It seemed that everything had to be done by *us* and had to be done *today*. We could

barely recover from the exhaustion of one day before we were called to face the next. We knew that we were getting older (our tiredness told us that) and that our life was passing quickly, but we had too much to do to worry about it. Life was rushing by and it seemed to demand that we spend more time dealing with the lives of others than in considering our own.

As we come to the end of the river of our life, it broadens and slows. We have time to sit and ponder what our life was, is, and will be. We still hunger for this life, but perhaps not with great passion. We realize that we are closer to the Falls than to the high peaks that marked our beginning, and we accept that. We still want to find some meaning in our waning days, to feel that we have not become superfluous. And we still want to be loved as we float through the last years of our life.

At last we come to the end of the river of our life. Rushing towards the twilight, our future is still hidden by the mist rising from the Great Falls ahead. The light grows dim, signalling that this life's day is almost over. Looking back, we can see children of the noon rushing about in their little boats, busy with business, new loves, new ventures. For us now all that seems far away. All is quiet as the tide of our life carries us along safe from any lingering rocks. It sweeps us along faster and faster, but quietly. It is almost as though we were in a moving pool of tremendous force. It inexorably rips us free of all our things, all our historic loves, until finally we stand naked and free of the past. All that is left to us is a swiftly diminishing present and an unending future.

At last we are drawn in by the final force of the Falls, and with a sigh of relief pass through the boundary that marks the end of our beginning. We break out of the last shadows of this life and enter that land where the light of an eternal day awaits us.

> This flowing life is finished.
> Our river has run its course.
> And we are happy.

Epilogue: Memories **34**

> Our experiences of this life have left footprints impressed on memory and these images are ever present to us even though the events have long passed.
>
> *On the Trinity,* 10.8.11

In this life the greatest gift we can give to each other is the gift of good memories. In this life only memories last. The gift of good memories can be given at any age. Whether we are just beginning, in the middle, or at the very end of the river of life, we leave "footprints" in the minds of others.

The very young give memories of days when life was fresh and sparkling. Looking into the face of a child smiling at its bright new world, we are reminded how our first and only day of eternity shall be.

Those in the prime of life (people like the college students I sometimes teach) remind us of how fine it is to be vigorous and strong. They remind us of how it was to really feel good, to be busy about doing important things with our lives. The vigorous young people rushing past us on the street remind us of how we shall feel on that first and only day of eternity.

And those in their last days, the very old or the very sick, give us perhaps the most important memory of all: the memory of how one can wait patiently for the coming of the Lord. They remind us that if only we have faith and don't give up, the Lord will come for us and take us home on that first and only day of eternity.

Jesus gives us good memories too. Indeed, that's why he came to us. Augustine correctly noted that God could have saved us in a million different ways, but only by becoming human could he *show* us how much he loved us, only by becoming human could he give us good memories. And very good memories he did indeed give us:

. . . the memory of a God who understands human happiness and who rejoiced to make wine at the wedding feast of a friend;

. . . the memory of a God who understands human sorrow and who knows how it feels to stand at the grave of a loved one and weep uncontrollably, because that's what he did at the grave of Lazarus;

. . . the memory of a God who understands when someone says: "I'm sorry, nothing more can be done. You must get ready to die," because he heard those same words from Pilate just before he was taken out to be crucified;

. . . the memory of a God who understands when a human prays: "O God, let this chalice of suffering pass from me!" because he said those same words in the Garden of Gethsemani and the suffering did *not* pass;

. . . the memory of a God who understands when a human prays: "O God! My God! Why have your forsaken me?" because he voiced that terrible cry himself a few hours before he died.

Indeed Jesus-God, through his life on earth, gave us some wondrous memories:

. . . the memory of a God who played with children;

. . . the memory of a God who went fishing with friends and did not catch anything;

. . . the memory of a God who forgave a poor sinner when humans surrounding her demanded her execution;

. . . the memory of a God who so desperately wanted to be with human beings that on the night before his execution, he took bread and wine, blessed it, broke it into pieces, and gave it to his friends saying: "Take and eat! This is my Body; this is my Blood. Do this in memory of me."

Jesus gave us all these memories in his lifetime and then he died. But then he came back to give us the most precious memory of all, the memory of what it is like to live after death:

. . . it is like the story of Emmaus, walking in the calm of evening along a country road with friends;

. . . it is like having a picnic on the beach (as Jesus did) with those who care about you;

. . . it is like having Jesus-God ask us (as he asked Peter): "Do you love me more than anything else?" and being able to answer honestly and without reservation perhaps for the first time in our lives: "Yes, Lord! You *know* that I love you!"

Jesus, by his life and death and resurrection, gave us good memories of what our human life is like just now and what our life can be in the future. He gave us good memories, and through these memories he gives us hope. He gives us the hope that we too can have success in our lives. And what shall be the measure of such success? Perhaps only this:

> to die, and have friends remember
> our passing with regret;
> to die, and have Jesus remember
> our lives with a smile.